DEER ON THE

Selected Poems

IAIN CRICHTON SMITH was born in Glasgow in 1928, but his father died of TB before he could know him, and his fiercely Calvinist mother took him back to her native Isle of Lewis in the Outer Hebrides. He grew up with his two brothers in the village of Bayble, where he spoke Gaelic, and not until he began school did English become necessary. He went to university in Aberdeen (it was the first time he had left the island) and after receiving his MA he joined the British Army Education Corps for his National Service. He then became a secondary school teacher in Clydebank, near Glasgow, and for twenty-two years at Oban High School. Much of his writing was done after work. His first book, *The Long River* (1955) was followed by *The White Noon* (1959), *Thistles and Roses* (1961), and the long poem, *Deer on the High Hills* (1962). Thereafter, collections in English or Gaelic appeared regularly, including several *Selected* editions, culminating in a *Collected Poems* in 1992 from Carcanet (Poetry Book Society Special Commendation) which was expanded and reissued as *New Collected Poems* in 2011.

JOHN GREENING (b.1954) has won several prizes for his poetry – notably, the Bridport, the *TLS* Centenary and the Arvon – and in 2008 he received a Cholmondeley Award from the Society of Authors. He has published over twenty collections, large and small, including *Heath* with Penelope Shuttle (Nine Arches, 2016). Carcanet have brought out both *To the War Poets* (2013) and *The Silence* (2019) which features his long Sibelius poem. In 2017 there was a memoir of his time in Egypt, *Threading a Dream* (Gatehouse). His most recent publications are the pamphlets *Europa's Flight* (New Walk, 2019), *Moments Musicaux* (Salzburg, 2020) and *a Post Card to* (Red Squirrel Press, 2020, with Stuart Henson).

CARCANET CLASSICS INCLUDE

Dictator/Gilgamesh adapted by Philip Terry
Gilgamesh Retold by Jenny Lewis
Pearl translated by Jane Draycott
Edmund Blunden, *Selected Poems* edited by Robyn Marsack
Catullus, *The Books of Catullus* translated by Simon Smith
Rebecca Elson, *A Responsibility to Awe: Collected Poems*
John Heath-Stubbs, *Selected Poems* edited by John Clegg
Walter Pater, *Selected Essays* edited by Alex Wong
Propertius, *Poems* translated by Patrick Worsnip
Arthur Rimbaud, *Illuminations* translated by John Ashbery
George Seferis, *Collected Poems* translated by Edmund Keeley and Philip Sherrard
Charles Tomlinson, *Swimming Chenango Lake: selected poems* edited by David Morley
William Carlos Williams, *Collected Poems, volumes I and II* edited by Walton Litz and Christopher MacGowan

IAIN CRICHTON SMITH

Deer on the High Hills

SELECTED POEMS

edited by

JOHN GREENING

CARCANET
CLASSICS

First published in Great Britain in 2021 by
Carcanet
Alliance House, 30 Cross Street
Manchester M2 7AQ
www.carcanet.co.uk

A CIP catalogue record for this book is available from the British Library.
ISBN 978 1 80017 094 0

Printed in Great Britain by SRP Ltd, Exeter, Devon

MIX
Paper from responsible sources
FSC® C014540

The publisher acknowledges financial assistance from Arts Council England.

Supported using public funding by
ARTS COUNCIL ENGLAND

CONTENTS

FOREWORD

The third and most recent *Selected Poems* by Iain Crichton Smith (1928–98) appeared in 1985, when his name was familiar from *The New Poetry* and Penguin Modern Poets. He is still well known in Scotland, where his Highland Clearances novel, *Consider the Lilies*, has been much used in the classroom; but since the 1992 *Collected* which he oversaw, and despite an invaluable revised *New Collected* (2011, ed. McGuire) his poetry has rather drifted out of focus. Certainly, the context in which a reader might encounter it now looks very different, more diverse, less exclusively male. But while other poets of his generation have been revived and celebrated (George Mackay Brown has had at least two biographies), there haven't been many voices speaking up for this particular islander. Seamus Heaney valued him enough to place him alongside Brown, Sorley MacLean and Norman MacCaig in his elegy 'Would They Had Stay'd'.* He points us to 'Deer on the High Hills' ('Iain's poem/Where sorrow just sits and rocks.'), Crichton Smith's own favourite, and undoubtedly his greatest achievement, which is why I have chosen it for the overall title.

In compiling a manageable selection for today's readers, I was faced with a number of challenges – chiefly, what to do about all the poems omitted from that very substantial *New Collected* (well over a hundred from books published in the 1970s alone) and those scattered elsewhere in magazines and anthologies which have never been reprinted. As Robin

* 'Would They Had Stay'd', *Electric Light* (Faber, 2001).

Fulton somewhat wistfully remarked in the introduction to an earlier *Selected* (whose launch in Dundee I was lucky enough to attend): 'prolific writers go on being prolific'. There were indeed many books to come after that 1981 Macdonald selection and the more streamlined one from Carcanet, although Crichton Smith was only seventy when he died: *A Life* (1986), *The Village and Other Poems* (1989), *Ends and Beginnings* (1994), *The Human Face* (1996), *The Leaf and the Marble* (1998) and the posthumous *A Country for Old Men & My Canadian Uncle* (2000). He wrote poems as one might skim pebbles on the sea, hoping one or two of them will take off.

I am immensely grateful for Matthew McGuire's scholarly edition, but the 1985 *Selected* remained my template, since it represents the poet's own choice. Yet I couldn't resist some pebble-hunting, so I also read all the original collections and found myself picking treasures from the sea-bed around Lewis. While respecting the poet-editor's judgment, the way he ensured there was a balance of light and dark, I have tried to bring a fresh (not necessarily Scottish) perspective for those who feel they already have the measure of Iain Crichton Smith, while maintaining some sort of chronology. My intention was to bring out certain facets he kept in the shadows, as well as highlighting the experimental late work, the broader reach, the more international outlook.

Iain Crichton Smith should be considered as a European writer rather than a 'Regional' one, which is how he was too often presented. Yes, he was shaped by the Isle of Lewis and its Calvinism, but only as Robert Lowell ('the poet I admire most and find closest to myself') was shaped by Boston. He had plenty to say about, for example, South Africa, Australia, Palestine, Rome, Renaissance art and the Russian Revolution, TV and love. He was often very funny, too. There is even a surrealist streak, especially among the several dozen poems here that didn't make it into the Carcanet *Selected* or the *New Collected.*

Since 'Iain Mac a'Ghobhainn' also wrote in Gaelic – as the troubling pun in the last line of 'Poem of Lewis' reminds us – I felt I could not exclude that side of his work; a *Selected Poems in English* would short-change the reader, and Crichton Smith's translations of Mac a'Ghobhainn are very fine. It seemed better to omit entirely his versions of Alexander Macdonald, Duncan Ban MacIntyre and Sorley MacLean which can be found in the *New Collected*, but would not flourish in these rather more cramped conditions. I was also obliged to drop some of the long poems, although I have found room for what Donald Tovey would have called 'bleeding chunks'.

John Greening

THE TEXT

The texts used are either from the 2011 *New Collected* or (since Matthew McGuire excluded certain poems) from the original individual collections. I have also used these as a guide to the running order, while trying to maintain the trajectory of the 1985 *Selected*. Punctuation varies between editions and I have opted for the least ambiguous, unless I felt the ambiguity was deliberate. Where there was any suggestion of an error or substantial later revision I have checked alternative printings and recordings, relying finally on those with which the poet himself was involved. While editors have usually retained Iain Crichton Smith's rather unconventional spellings of Michelangelo and Bruegel, I have chosen not to.

ACKNOWLEDGEMENTS

I am grateful to the following individuals for help in preparing this selection: Gerry Cambridge, James Campbell, Niall Campbell, Jane Greening, Robyn Marsack, Christopher Reid, Stephen Rogers, Fraser Steel, and also to The National Poetry Library.

DEER ON THE HIGH HILLS

Selected Poems

POEM OF LEWIS

Here they have no time for the fine graces
of poetry, unless it freely grows
in deep compulsion, like water in the well,
woven into the texture of the soil
in a strong pattern. They have no rhymes
to tailor the material of thought
and snap the thread quickly on the tooth.
One would have thought that this black north
was used to lightning, crossing the sky like fish
swift in their element. One would have thought
the barren rock would give a value to
the bursting flower. The two extremes,
mourning and gaiety, meet like north and south
in the one breast, milked by knuckled time,
till dryness spreads across each ageing bone.
They have no place for the fine graces
of poetry. The great forgiving spirit of the word
fanning its rainbow wing, like a shot bird
falls from the windy sky. The sea heaves
in visionless anger over the cramped graves
and the early daffodil, purer than a soul,
is gathered into the terrible mouth of the gale.

‘SOME DAYS WERE RUNNING LEGS’

Some days were running legs and joy
and old men telling tomorrow would be
a fine day surely: for sky was red
at setting of sun between the hills.

Some nights were parting at the gates
with day’s companions: and dew falling
on heads clear of ambition except light
returning and throwing stones at sticks.

Some days were rain flooding forever the green
pasture: and horses turning to the wind
bare smooth backs. The toothed rocks rising
sharp and grey out of the ancient sea.

Some nights were shawling mirrors lest the lightning
strike with the eel’s speed out of the storm.
Black the roman rocks came from the left squawking
and the evening flowed back around their wings.

STATEMENT BY A RESPONSIBLE SPINSTER

It was my own kindness brought me here
to an eventless room, bare of ornament.
This is the threshold charity carried me over.
I live here slowly in a permanent

but clement weather. It will do for ever.
A barren bulb creates my firmament.
A sister cries: 'I might have learned to wear
sardonic jewellery and the lineament

of a fine beauty, fateful and austere.
I might have trained my perilous armament
on the learnèd and ferocious. A lover
would have emerged uniquely from that element.'

I know that for a lie, product of fever.
This is my beginning. Justice meant
that a man or woman who succumbs to fear
should not be married to good merriment.

I inspect justice through a queer air.
Indeed he lacks significant ornament.
Nevertheless he does not laugh or suffer
though, like pity's cruelty, he too is permanent.

And since I was trapped by pity and the clever
duplicities of age, my last emolument
returns, thus late, its flat incurious stare
on my ambiguous love, my only monument.

FOR THE UNKNOWN SEAMEN OF THE 1939–45 WAR BURIED IN IONA CHURCHYARD

One would like to be able to write something for them
not for the sake of the writing but because
a man should be named in dying as well as living,
in drowning as well as on death-bed, and because
the brain being brain must try to establish laws.

Yet these events are not amenable
to any discipline that we can impose
and are not in the end even imaginable.
What happened was simply this, bad luck for those
who have lain here twelve years in a changing pose.

These things happen and there's no explaining,
and to call them 'chosen' might abuse a word.
It is better also not to assume a mourning,
moaning stance. These may have well concurred
in whatever suddenly struck them through the absurd

or maybe meaningful. One simply doesn't
know enough, or understand what came
out of the altering weather in a fashioned
descriptive phrase that was common to each name
or may have surrounded each like a dear frame.

Best not to make much of it and leave these seamen
in the equally altering acre they now have
inherited from strangers though yet human.
They fell from sea to earth from grave to grave
and, griefless now, taught others how to grieve.

THE WINDOW

We walked that night between the piled houses.
It was late and cold. Frost gleamed on the road
like the sheen of over-learning. Beaked and bowed,
the lamp-posts lectured light, dispensed discourses.

All windows were dark. As on the edge of a cliff
we warily walked, stepping on steeps of silence
except for the click-click-click of our heels, the parlance
of stones that down a well make a crooked graph.

A bus like a late planet turned a corner.
There was nothing else, we and darkness merely.
These ancient houses had never stood in an early
atmosphere or radiance of summer.

At day's end they sank heavily into slumber
as a man sleeps open-mouthed at his fire when
too much light and heat exhaust his brain.
He floats on darkness like a tired swimmer.

None but we two, walking almost as over
a world's end. Yellow light sang and sang
into our coats, our faces, skin and tongue.
We thought each other shook with a yellow fever.

Then she said: 'Look, there's a light up there'
and, slowly climbing the cliff-face, my eyes came
to a square light that shone with a blunt flame.
It was solid and dull and red in the yellow air.

And I wondered whose it was – a sleepless man
turning and turning between a window and bed
cursing his sleeplessness and the huge dread
shrill light that pecked at his bemused brain?

Or was it perhaps one studious and grave
who, grasping his pale book, would listen to
the sound it made, the authentic echo
of words returning what he thought and gave?

Or was it a mother, waking for her child,
who could not sleep because of the cold air,
and stumbled between dull bed and dull chair
in the red light imperious and wild?

At least the light was human: and we looked
into each other's eyes shyly as if
a house had suddenly sprung from a dead cliff
and it was all our searching spirits lacked.

OLD WOMAN

And she, being old, fed from a mashed plate
as an old mare might droop across a fence
to the dull pastures of its ignorance.
Her husband held her upright while he prayed

to God who is all-forgiving to send down
some angel somewhere who might land perhaps
in his foreign wings among the gradual crops.
She munched, half dead, blindly searching the spoon.

Outside, the grass was raging. There I sat
imprisoned in my pity and my shame
that men and women having suffered time
should sit in such a place, in such a state

and wished to be away, yes, to be far away
with athletes, heroes, Greek or Roman men
who pushed their bitter spears into a vein
and would not spend an hour with such decay.

'Pray God,' he said, 'we ask you, God,' he said.
The bowed back was quiet. I saw the teeth
tighten their grip around a delicate death.
And nothing moved within the knotted head

but only a few poor veins as one might see
vague wishless seaweed floating on a tide
of all the salty waters where had died
too many waves to mark two more or three.

LUSS VILLAGE

Such walls, like honey, and the old are happy
in morphean air like goldfish in a bowl.
Ripe roses trail their margins down a sleepy
mediaeval treatise on the slumbering soul.

And even the water, fabulously silent,
has no salt tales to tell us, nor makes jokes
about the yokel mountains, huge and patient,
that will not court her but read shadowy books.

A world so long departed! In the churchyard
the tilted tombs still gossip, and the leaves
of stony testaments are read by Richard,
Jean and Carol, pert among the sheaves

of unscythed shadows, while the noon day hums
with bees and water and the ghosts of psalms.

A NOTE ON PURITANS

There was no curtain between them and fire.
Every moment was a moment when
a man could sink into a tranced despair
or shake his heels to vanity and turn
with frenzied gaiety from that drying air.

Therefore their urgency. That fire glowed
along their blackened senses, hour by hour.
Only the book they clutched so tightly cheered
hearts that might stop, eyes that their burning fear
could hole with flame: heads that their thoughts had charred.

Garden and gardener, book and reader glowed:
limbs crackled their sins: silks twitched in a blue flame:
a man's flesh melted in the mouth of God:
he lost his name to earn a lasting name.
A heaven flashed where all that oil flowed.

That was great courage to have watched that fire,
not placing a screen before it as we do
with pictures, poems, landscapes, a great choir
of mounting voices which can drown the raw
hissing and spitting of flame with other fire.

That was great courage to have stayed as true
to truth as man can stay. From them we learn
how certain truths can make men brutish too:
how few can watch the bared teeth slow-burn
and not be touched by the lumps of fire they chew

into contempt and barrenness. I accuse
these men of singleness and loss of grace
who stared so deeply into the fire's hues
that all was fire to them.
                                                  Yes, to this place
they should return. Cheeks have the fire men choose.

DYING IS NOT SETTING OUT

Dying is not setting out
in a full flower of sails.
More complex ropes are taut
across the blue pulse.

Dying is not like sailing
by the shores of Mull or
Tiree. Sheet's less willing
and twists in thick air.

It's not for Skye we make.
Not with simple hands
use south wind for luck.
We wear our islands

unconnected in spite of
intellect's glittering stride.
We sail into the grave
of the more than dead.

GIRL WITH ORANGE SUNSHADE

An orange sunshade wheels about her head.
The sunshade shading sun is yet a sun
mimicked by colour, halo of the red
and mild attendant of the coloured bone.

Yet it is mimic as if the other sun
should not attack her, being saved by this
paper not passion which she learns to spin
as if herself were Fortune, pert-faced miss.

And this cool wheel about her ordered hair
is like the art we nourish in our rooms
on little water and a jar of air.
It holds us steady from the searing flames.
We mimic fire to shield us from the fire
and shade our heads with bright and paper poems.

SUNDAY MORNING WALK

Sunday of wrangling bells – and salt in the air –
I passed the tall black men and their women walking
over the tight-locked streets which were all on fire
with summer ascendant. The seas were talking and talking

as I took my way to the wood where the river ran quiet.
The grass lay windowed in sunlight, the leaves were raging
in furious dying green. The road turned right
round the upstanding castle whose stone unageing

marks how a world remains as I being now
pack of a wandering flesh take holiday strolling
far from the churches' declaiming. Health will allow
riots of naiads and nymphs, so wantonly rolling

with me in leaves in woods, thinking how once
Jove took his pleasure of Leda or – splendid embracing –
god would mate with a goddess – rapid the pounce,
fruitful the hot-thighed meeting, no need for unlacing.

And occupied thus, I came where a dead sheep lay
close to a fence, days gone. The flies were hissing and buzzing
out of the boiling eyes, wide open as day.
I stood in the sunlight beside it, watching and musing.

Three crows famished yards off. Live sheep grazed far
from the rotting carcass. The jaw, well-shaved, lay slackly
there on the warm quiet grass. The household air
was busy with buzzing like fever. How quickly, how quickly

the wool was peeled from the back. How still was the flesh.
How the visiting flies would not knock at the door of the sockets.
How the hole in the side gaped red, a well-sized gash.
How the clear young lambs grazed in the shade of the thickets.

And the sun blazed hot on my shoulder. Here was no shade.
But the sheep was quiet, so quiet. There was nothing to notice
but the grape-bunched flies and the crows. Could a world have stayed
if I'd taken a stick in my hand and beat off the flies?

They would merely return when I'd gone and busy as always
inhabit this larder again, no matter how brightly
I struck with my smart sharp stick. All I could praise –
yes, all I could praise – was the sheep lying there so quietly

not knowing not knowing. High summer was raging around.
I stood in my slack clean clothes. The stones were burning.
The flies in the wound continued their occupied sound
as I turned my back on a death of no weeping or mourning.

BY FERRY TO THE ISLAND

We crossed by ferry to the bare island
where sheep and cows stared coldly through the wind –
the sea behind us with its silver water,
the silent ferryman standing in the stern
clutching his coat about him like old iron.

We landed from the ferry and went inland
past a small church down to the winding shore
where a white seagull fallen from the failing
chill and ancient daylight lay so pure
and softly breasted that it made more dear

the lesser white around us. There we sat
sheltered by a rock beside the sea.
Someone made coffee, someone played the fool
in a high rising voice for two hours.
The sea's language was more grave and harsh.

And one sat there whose dress was white and cool.
The fool sparkled his wit that she might hear
new diamonds turning on her naked finger.
What might the sea think or the dull sheep
lifting its head through heavy Sunday sleep?

And later, going home, a moon rising
at the end of a cart-track, minimum of red,
the wind being dark, imperfect cows staring
out of their half-intelligence, and a plough
lying on its side in the cold, raw

naked twilight, there began to move
slowly, like heavy water, in the heart
the image of the gull and of that dress,
both being white and out of the darkness rising
the moon ahead of us with its rusty ring.

CULLODEN AND AFTER

You understand it? How they returned from Culloden
over the soggy moors aslant, each cap
at the low ebb no new full tide could pardon:
how they stood silent at the end of the rope
unwound from battle: and to the envelope
of a bedded room came home, polite and sudden.

And how, much later, bards from Tiree and Mull
would write of exile in the hard town
where mills belched English, anger of new school:
how they remembered where the sad and brown
landscapes were dear and distant as the crown
that fuddled Charles might study in his ale.

There was a sleep. Long fences leaned across
the vacant croft. The silly cows were heard
mooing their sorrow and their Gaelic loss.
The pleasing thrush would branch upon a sword.
A mind withdrew against its dreamed hoard
as whelks withdraw or crabs their delicate claws.

And nothing to be heard but songs indeed
while wandering Charles would on his olives feed
and from his Minch of sherries mumble laws.

A YOUNG HIGHLAND GIRL STUDYING POETRY

Poetry drives its lines into her forehead
like an angled plough across a bare field.
I've seen her kind before, of the live and dead
who bore humped creels when the beating winds were wild.

Nor did they know much poetry but were skilful
at healing children, bringing lambs to birth.
The earth they lived from did not make them soulful.
The foreign rose abated at their mouth.

Yet they were dancers too and feared the season
when 'pale Orion shook the seas with fire'.
Peculiar waters had their inner reasons
for curing wastrels of a mental star.

And she – like them – should grow along these valleys
bearing bright children, being kind to love.
Simple affection needs no complex solace
nor quieter minds abstractions of the grave.

For most must walk though some by natural flying
learn from the bitter winds a kind of praise.
These fruits are different. She will know one dying
but he by many deaths will bless her days.

from LILAC, SNOW AND SHADOW

A lilac dress casting a long shadow
on a patch of bright snow.
The skies pass by in blue, in blue marching.

O dear my country that you give me these,
lilac on snow, the urgent turbulent skies,
me walking at ease the supple air inhaling.

O dear my island with the seas around you
I kneel this moment to the innumerable dead,
who have fed dense waters and the blue Aprils,

for these simplicities of a complex air,
a lilac dress, the snow, the blue sky marching,
myself of a hundred colours swarming there.

HOME

To have to stay
in spite of scorn, hatred,
in spite of shattered
illusions also. To be unable
to break cleanly away
since this is truly home
simple imperishable
since otherwhere is chill,
dull-breasted, dumb.

Since this too is hated,
loved, willed to be perfect, willed
to a finer yield
fiercer, less barren, richer,
its harvests be completed.
Since to have seen tall men
moving in light and fire
yet human too is more
grace than can be given

this (one says) is tragic
(to be fixed on a wheel
implacable, internal,
as tears break. As roses,
bowed gravely down to rock,
proliferate endless versions.)
Is not tragic but cause
of fresh honours, horses
impelled by used reins.

DEER ON THE HIGH HILLS

I

A deer looks through you to the other side,
and what it is and sees is an inhuman pride.

II

Yesterday three deer stood at the roadside.
It was icy January and there they were
like debutantes on a smooth ballroom floor.

They stared at us out of that French
arrogant atmosphere, like Louis the Sixteenth
sustained in twilight on a marble plinth.

They wore the inhuman look of aristocrats
before a revolution comes, and the people
blaspheme the holy bells in the high steeple.

Before the ice breaks, and heroes in spring
come up like trees with bursting wrongs in their arms
and feed the nobles to the uniform worms.

So were these deer, balanced on delicate logic,
till suddenly they broke from us and went
outraged and sniffing into the dark wind.

Difficult to say where they go to
in the harsh weather when the mountains stand
like judging elders, tall on either hand.

Except that they know the ice is breaking now.
They take to the hills pursued by darkness and lie
beneath the starry metaphysical sky.

Sometimes in a savage winter they'll come down
and beg like fallen nobles for their bread.
They'd rather live in poverty than be dead.

Nevertheless there's something dangerous
in a deer's head. He might suddenly open your belly
with his bitter antlers to the barren sky.

Especially in winter when tormented
by loneliness they descend to this road
with great bounding leaps like the mind of God.

In summer they can be ignored. They crop so gently
among the hills that no one notices
their happy heads sunk in the feeding cresses.

But beware of them now when ice is on the ground.
A beggared noble can conceal a sword
next to his skin for the aimless and abhorred

tyrants who cannot dance but throw stones,
tyrants who can crack the finest bones:
tyrants who do not wear but break most ancient crowns.

III

One would be finished with these practical things
in order to return as deer do
to the tall mountain springs.

Nevertheless one should not so return
till soldier of the practical or doer
one wholly learns to learn

a real contempt, a fine hard-won disdain
for these possessions, marbles of unripe children,
as, again,

a deer might walk along a sweating street
stare in a cramped window and then go
back to the hills but not on ignorant feet.

IV

Forget these purple evenings and these poems
that solved all or took for myth
the pointed sail of Ulysses enigmatic.

There was Hector with his child in his arms.
Where is that other Hector
who wore the internal shield, the inner sword?

Ulysses scurries, like a rat trapped in a maze.
He wears the sharp look of a business magnate.
Late from the office he had a good excuse.

Ideas clash on the mountain tops.
By the appalled peaks the deer roar.
Simply a question of rutting, these cloudy systems

or as yesterday we saw a black cloud
become the expression of a tall mountain.
And that was death, the undertaker, present.

And all became like it for that moment,
assumption of anguish, and the hollow waters
the metaphysics of an empty country

deranged, deranged, a land of rain and stones
of stones and rain, of the huge barbarous bones,
plucked like a loutish harp their harmonies.

V

You must build from the rain and stones,
from the incurable numbers: the grasses
innumerable on the many hills.

Not to geometry or algebra,
or an inhuman music, but
in the hollow roar of the waterfall,

you must build from there and not be
circumvented by sunlight or a taste of love
or intuitions from the sky above

the deadly rock. Or even history.
Prince Charles in a gay Highland shawl,
or mystery in a black Highland coffin.

You must build from the rain and stones
till you can make
a stylish deer on the high hills,
and let its leaps be unpredictable!

VI

Duncan Ban MacIntyre, the poet,
knew them intimately, was one of them.
They had waxen hides, they were delicate dancers.

They evolved their own music which became
his music: they elected him
their poet laureate.

It was a kind of Eden these days
with something Cretan in his eulogy.
Nevertheless he shot them also.

Like shooting an image or a vivid grace.
Brutality and beauty danced together
in a silver air, incorruptible.

And the clean shot did not disturb his poems.
Nor did the deer kneel in a pool of tears.
The stakes were indeed high in that game.

And the rocks did not weep with sentiment.
They were simply there: the deer were simply there.
The witty gun blazed from his knowing hand.

VII

What is the knowledge of the deer?
Is there a philosophy of the hills?
Do their heads peer into the live stars?

Do rumours of death disturb them? They do not live
by local churchyards, hotels or schools.
They inhabit wild systems.

Do they outface winds or lie down
in warm places? Winter, interrogant,
displaces spring and summer, undulant.

Their horns have locked in blood. Yes, their horns
have gored bellies. The dainty hind
has absolute passion, similar and proud.

It is not evil makes the horns bright
but a running natural lustre. The blood
is natural wounding. Metaphoric sword

is not their weapon, but an honest thrust.
Nor does the moon affect their coupling, nor
remonstrant gods schoolmaster their woods.

Evil not intentional, but desire
disturbs to battle. The great spring is how
these savage captains tear to indigo

the fiery guts. Evil's more complex, is
a languaged metaphor, like the mists that scarf
the deadly hind and her bewildered calf.

VIII

Supposing God had a branched head like this
considering Himself in a pool.
It is not the image of the beautiful

makes it so, simply as in a mirror,
but in its fadingness, as on the ice
the deer might suddenly slip, go suddenly under,

their balance being precarious. It is this,
that makes her beautiful, she who now obscures
unconscious heavens with her conscious ray,

is concourse of bright flesh, sad, is remembering
herself so going, so implacable,
her failing voyages to the obstinate rocks:

as deer so stand, precarious, of a style,
half-here, half-there, a half-way lustre breaking
a wise dawn in a chained ocean far.

As dear, so dear, Vesuvius, rocket, you
being ice and water, winter and summer, take
the mountainous seas into your small logic.

God may not be beautiful, but you
suffer a local wound. You bleed to death
from all that's best, your active anima.

The deer and you may well be beautiful,
for through your bones as through a mathematics
concordant honouring beauty richly breaks.

IX

Deer on the high peaks, calling, calling,
you speak of love, love of the mind and body.
Your absolute heads populate the hills

like daring thoughts, half-in, half-out this world.
As a lake might open, and a god peer
into a room where failing darkness glows.

Deer on the high peaks, there have been heads
as proud as yours, destructive, ominous,
of an impetuous language, measureless.

Heads like yours, so scrutinous and still,
yet venomed too with the helpless thrust of spring,
so magisterial, violent, yet composed:

heads of a thirsty intellect, sensuous as
the thirst of bellies in a summer day
July and waspish, on a murmuring ground.

Heads like valleys where the stars fed
unknown and magical, strange and unassuaged,
the harmonies humming in a green place.

So proud these heads, original, distinct,
they made an air imperial around
their pointed scrutiny, passionate with power.

Electric instinct of the high hills
till later later peasants in the valleys
felt in their bones disquieting kingdoms break

and matrons, by small cottages, would sense
implacable navies in their native wombs,
a generation of a harder wit

and later later when the senses quickened
(the hills being bare again) in a new season
in a night honoured with a desperate star

another head appeared, fiercer than these,
disdain flashed from his horns, a strange cry
perplexed the peasants, somnolent, appeased.

X

Deer on the high peaks, the wandering senses
are all, are all: fanatic heads deceive,
like branches springing in a true desert.

Smell now the cresses and the winter root,
passage of heather, journey of rank fox
mortal and moving on the strange hills.

In spring the raven and lascivious swallow,
migrant of air, the endless circle closing,
unclosing, closing, a bewildering ring

of natural marriage, pagan, sensuous.
Return of seasons, and the fugitive
Culloden of scents, erratic, hesitant.

The snow returning, and the summer wasp
more caustic than idea, hum of bees
at their devotions to the wild honey.

The hind crowned with her wanton sex,
rage of the sap in trees, the urgent salmon
pregnant with oceans dying into streams.

And these return in spite of the idea,
the direct reasoning road, the mad Ulysses
so unperverted, so implacable,

so wearing late his dull ironic crown
among a people he has never loved
nor felt in boredom kinship ominous

but fixed on a reasoned star his obstinate gaze
who came at last to where his childhood was
an infant island in an ancient place.

XI

Deer on the high peaks, let me turn
my gaze far from you, where the river winds
its slow way like an old man's argument.

The rocks obstinate, the rains persistent,
the stones ingathered into their chastened fury,
all things themselves, a fierce diversity.

The rampant egos of the flat plains,
the thorns gentle with their sour flowers,
tongues of the sharp stones, the water's business.

Contorted selves that twist in a dark wind,
far from the mountains, from the far and clear
ordered inventions of the stars ongoing.

And here, below, the water's business
smoothing the stone, consenting to the heads
that, easy of a summer, stare and stare

and speak: 'I am, I am. Preserve me, O preserve.
Make me in mirror matchless and the earl
of such imagined kingdoms as endure.

I pray, I pray, a marchioness of this
dismembered kingdom, let my face be seen
not mortal now but of a lasting grace.'

Roar of the waters, prickly thrust of thorn,
immutable stone, sand of a brute fact,
these are the maenads of necessity.

And the deer look down, Platonic dawn breaks
on Highland hills as distant as a thought,
an excellent Athens, obstinate mirage,

while the stone rears, the venomed stone rears
its savage being, and the waters pour
illusive summers to the real seas,

while the deer stand imperious, of a style,
make vibrant music, high and rich and clear,
mean what the plain mismeans, inform a chaos.

XII

Deer on the high hills, in your halfway kingdom,
uneasy in this, uneasy in the other,
but all at ease when earth and sky together

are mixed are mixed, become a royalty
none other knows, neither the migrant birds
nor the beasts chained to their instinctive courses.

That halfway kingdom is your royalty
you on a meditative truth impaled
the epicures of feeding absolutes

you of a metaphysics still and proud
native to air, native to earth both,
indigenous deer beneath a cloudburst sky:

to whom the lightning's native and the thunder,
whose sockets flash with an annunciant fire,
whose storms are vegetation's dearest friend.

Your antlers flash in light, your speed like thought
is inspiration decorous and assured
a grace not theological but of

accomplished bodies, sensuous and swift,
of summer scents enjoyers, and of winters
the permanent spirits, watchful, unappeased:

of summer hills a speaking radiance,
the body's language, excellent and pure,
discoursing love, free as the wandering wind:

of scentless winters the philosophers,
vigilant always like a tiptoe mind
on peaks of sorrow, brave and scrutinous:

on peaks of sorrow, brave and scrutinous,
on breakneck peaks, coherent and aplomb,
the image silent on the high hill.

XIII

Do colours cry? Does 'black' weep for the dead?
Is green so bridal, and is red the flag
and eloquent elegy of a martial sleep?

Are hills 'majestic' and devoted stones
plotting in inner distances our fall?
The mind a sea: and she a Helen who

in budding hours awakens to her new
enchanting empire all the summer day,
the keys of prisons dangling in her hands?

Is night a woman, and the moon a queen
or dowager of grace, and all the stars
archaic courtiers round ambiguous smiles?

Are rivers stories, and are plains their prose?
Are fountains poetry? And are rainbows the
wistful smiles upon a dying face?

And you, the deer, who walk upon the peaks,
are you a world away, a language distant?
Such symbols freeze upon my desolate lips!

XIV

There is no metaphor. The stone is stony.
The deer step out in isolated air.
We move at random on an innocent journey.

The rain is rainy and the sun is sunny.
The flower is flowery and the sea is salty.
My friend himself, himself my enemy.

The deer step out in isolated air.
Not nobles now but of a further journey.
Their flesh is distant as the air is airy.

The rivers torrents, and the grasses many.
The stars are starry, and the night nocturnal.
The fox a tenant of no other skin.

Who brings reports? There's one head to the penny.
A door is wooden, and no window grieves
for lovers turned away, for widows lonely.

The deer step out in isolated air.
The cloud is cloudy and the word is wordy.
Winter is wintry, lonely is your journey.

'You called sir did you?' 'I who was so lonely
would speak with you: would speak to this tall chair,
would fill it chock-full of my melancholy.'

So being lonely I would speak with any
stone or tree or river. Bear my journey
you endless water, dance with a human joy.

This distance deadly! God or goddess throw me
a rope to landscape, let that hill, so bare,
blossom with grapes, the wine of Italy.

The deer step out in isolated air.
Forgive the distance, let the transient journey
on delicate ice not tragical appear

for stars are starry and the rain is rainy,
the stone is stony, and the sun is sunny,
the deer step out in isolated air.

OLD WOMAN

Your thorned back
heavily under the creel
you steadily stamped the rising daffodil.

Your set mouth
forgives no one, not even God's justice
perpetually drowning law with grace.

Your cold eyes
watched your drunken husband come
unsteadily from Sodom home.

Your grained hands
dandled full and sinful cradles.
You built for your children stone walls.

Your yellow hair
burned slowly in a scarf of grey
wildly falling like the mountain spray.

Finally you're alone
among the unforgiving brass,
the slow silences, the sinful glass.

Who never learned,
not even ageing, to forgive
our poor journey and our common grave

while the free daffodils
wave in the valleys and on the hills
the deer look down with their instinctive skills,

and the huge sea
in which your brothers drowned sings slow
over the headland and the peevish crow.

TWO GIRLS SINGING

It neither was the words nor yet the tune.
Any tune would have done and any words.
Any listener or no listener at all.

As nightingales in rocks or a child crooning
in its own world of strange awakening
or larks for no reason but themselves.

So on the bus through late November running
by yellow lights tormented, darkness falling,
the two girls sang for miles and miles together

and it wasn't the words or tune. It was the singing.
It was the human sweetness in that yellow,
the unpredicted voices of our kind.

LENIN

In a chair of iron
sits coldly my image of Lenin,
that troubling man
'who never read a book for pleasure alone.'

The germ inside the sealed train
emerged, spread in wind and rain
into new minds in revolution
seeming more real than had been

for instance Dostoevsky. No, I can
romanticise no more that 'head of iron'
'the thought and will unalterably one'
'the world-doer,' 'thunderer,' 'the stone

rolling through clouds'. Simple to condemn
the unsymmetrical, simple to condone
that which oneself is not. By admiration
purge one's envy of unadult iron

when the true dialectic is to turn
in the infinitely complex, like a chain
we steadily burn through, steadily forge and burn
not to be dismissed in any poem

by admiration for the ruthless man
nor for the saint but for the moving on
into the endlessly various, real, human,
world which is no new era, shining dawn.

THE ARGUMENT

Our world is not predestined. So he chose
or did not choose to argue, being him.
And I being me in an excited pose
argued for our destiny, the trim
tracks that contain us, but he all aflame

spoke of the clear nobility of the soul,
himself both proud and noble. I replied
with words imperfectly in my control
how the will drives us, we undeified
unfree even for honour. He from pride

repelled such low dishonour. I appealed
to his pure passion, in a passionate tone
as if myself were suffering from guilt
but he quite calmly answered: 'We are known
to no one else.' I answered: 'The cold stone

suffers its gravity, and why should we
assume such freedom of the phantom skies.
We are a part of sad eternity.'
But he then honestly with flashing eyes
as if by grace and not the law replied:

'We are no stones. How could we speak of this
unvaried destiny if this were true?'
I did not listen to hypothesis
but watched his face where passion through and through
showed grace more varied than his reason knew,

a coiling of the spirit working there,
a human anguish of the beating soul,
and knew at last, had I not known before,
the struggle's what we live by, not the whole
unknown completion. I could humbly kneel

to such humanity predestined too,
noble behaviour of the best we are,
restless and proud, to abstract passion true.
Some world takes notice of the best and rare
as I of him, a passion of our star.

JOHNSON IN THE HIGHLANDS

A reasoning mind travels through this country.
In these sad wastes a Londoner by choice
sees water falling, and some meagre deer.

Examines with his tough reasoning mind
lochs, deer, and people: is not seduced
by Mrs Radcliffe's green hysteria

from a musical prose we've never once achieved,
whose fences cannot reach between the words
whose arguments are broken-backed with exile.

A classical sanity considers Skye.
A huge hard light falls across shifting hills.
This mind, contemptuous of miracles

and beggarly sentiment, illuminates
a healthy moderation. But I hear
like a native dog notes beyond his range

the modulations of a queer music
twisting his huge black body in the pain
that shook him also in raw blazing London.

THE CLEARANCES

The thistles climb the thatch. Forever
this sharp scale in our poems,
as also the waste music of the sea.

The stars shine over Sutherland
in a cold ceilidh of their own,
as, in the morning, the silver cane

cropped among corn. We will remember this.
Though hate is evil we cannot
but hope your courtier's heels in hell

are burning: that to hear
the thatch sizzling in tanged smoke
your hot ears slowly learn.

'IT IS THE OLD'

It is the old
who get up in the night to build the fires for the young.
Their gods, they imagine, are disposed
in a leisurely lazy heaven and prolong
a Norman sleep against the cold
and bitter frost.

And so they set
a delicate structure of sticks, enfolded in this
fear of their power, idolatry of their poise.
Not knowing in Saxon dawns how the abyss
their precarious tilt of sticks steadily lights
is what their boys

dread in their beds,
while dreaming of lords they can serve
of brilliance courage and wit.
Roads are built on each nerve –
Roman and servile and powerful. Their needs
point to the fire in the night.

AT THE FIRTH OF LORNE

In the cold orange light we stared across
to Mull and Kerrera and far Tiree.
A setting sun emblazoned your bright knee
to a brilliant gold to match your hair's gold poise.

Nothing had changed: the world was as it was
a million years ago. The slaty stone
slept in its tinged and aboriginal iron.
The sky might flower a little, and the grass

perpetuate its sheep. But from the sea
the bare bleak islands rose, beyond the few
uneasy witticisms we let pursue
their desolate silences. There was no tree

nor other witness to the looks we gave
each other there, inhuman as if tolled
by some huge bell of iron and of gold,
I no great Adam and you no bright Eve.

THE LAW AND THE GRACE

It's law they ask of me and not grace.
'Conform,' they say, 'your works are not enough.
Be what we say you should be' even if
graceful hypocrisy obscures my face.

'We know no angels. If you say you do
that's blasphemy and devilry.' Yet I have
known some bright angels, of spontaneous love.
Should I deny them, be to falsehood true,

the squeeze of law which has invented torture
to bring the grace to a malignant head?
Do you want me, angels, to be wholly dead?
Do you need, black devils, steadfastly to cure

life of itself? And you to stand beside
the stone you set on me? No, I have angels. Mine
are free and perfect. They have no design
on anyone else, but only on my pride

my insufficiency, imperfect works.
They often leave me but they sometimes come
to judge me to the core, till I am dumb.
Is this not law enough, you patriarchs?

HUME

More than this I do not love you,
Hume of the reasonable mind.
There was an otter crossed the sound,
a salmon in his cold teeth.

The mist came down. Between two capes
there was no road. There was a French
salon, an adoring wench.
He picked the salmon with his teeth.

Delicate Hume who swims through all
the daring firths of broken Scotland,
there were no roads across the land.
The causes, like old fences, yawned

gravely over wit and port.
Diplomacies are what displace
the inner law, the inner grace,
the Corryvreckan of bad art.

RYTHM

They dunno how it is. I smack a ball
right through the goals. But they dunno how the words
get muddled in my head, get tired somehow.
I look through the window, see. And there's a wall
I'd kick the ball against, just smack and smack.
Old Jerry he can't play, he don't know how,
not now at any rate. He's too flicking small.
See him in shorts, out in the crazy black.
Rythm, he says, and ryme. See him at back.
He don't know nuthing about Law. He'd fall
flat on his face, just like a big sack,
when you're going down the wing, the wind behind you
and crossing into the goalmouth, and they're roaring
the whole great crowd. They're up on their feet cheering.
The ball's at your feet and there it goes, just crack.
Old Jerry dives – the wrong way. And they're jearing
and I run to the centre and old Bash
jumps up and down, and I feel great, and wearing
my gold and purpel strip, fresh from the wash.

ENCOUNTER IN A SCHOOL CORRIDOR

Supposing today walking along this passage
in a flicker of gown Death were to turn and look
with his white skull face, raising his eyes from his book,
and I were to stare directly into that visage

which is almost over-learned and frightened too
as if to say: 'Surely not you as well.'
In this hygienic place without sound or smell
what would I, late cold Roman, say or do

but this perhaps: 'Always there was correction.
After the Fall, the careless summer leaves
must learn strict order, for the heart deceives
by wayward and incurious affection.

And the seasons always begin. There is no end
to the iron ring of law, the field of grace
whose shadows slant before the footballers.'
He then might show some pity as he turned

to face me down the dim-lit corridor
his arms so piled with books, face grained with thought,
and his slow legs remembering that riot
of flowering shadows and that youthful force.

THE CHESS PLAYER

When the badness came he was playing chess again.
'Someone most dear to you,' they said, 'has died.'
He scouted round the board and picked the queen.
(What use are bishops, knights?) 'We found,' they cried,
'your brother dead. His wounds were in the side.'

'Not in the head?' he said, not looking up.
'In the head and heart as well,' they answered. He
moved the tall queen delicately as in hope
but the king escaped again. 'Did he say of me
anything hopeful?' he asked savagely,

moving a pawn, his head carved to the wood
the king was carved from. 'No,' they said. '"Please tell
my brother this. Tell him I've understood
a very little." That's what he told us.' 'Well,
the chessboard tells me what of heaven or hell

I need to know and that's too much,' he cried,
shifting the queen. (The king escaped again.)
He smiled a little with the jaunty pride
one sometimes notices in desperate men.
'You see,' he said, 'when you came in just then

I had a vision of that very board.
They do not know, you see, none of them knows.
They're all quite evidently so far apart.
What do they know of each other? I dispose –
but each is wooden, in archaic pose.'

And then they saw (each one standing beside
the terrible trivial wrestler) with a start
that someone most dear to him indeed had died,
and stared at him grappling with his mental art,
and carefully made ready to depart.

ENVOI

Remember me when you come into your kingdom.
Remember me, beggar of mirrors, when you are confirmed
in the sleep of fulfilment on the white pillow.

Remember me who knock at the window,
who hirple on my collapsing stick, and know
the quivering northern lights of nerves.

Remember me in your good autumn.
I in my plates of frost go
among the falling crockery of hills

stones, plains, all falling and falling.
In my winter of the sick glass remember
me in your autumn, in your good sleep.

THE DEPARTING ISLAND

Strange to see it – how as we lean over
this vague rail, the island goes away
into its loved light grown suddenly foreign:
how the ship slides outward like a cold ray
from a sun turned cloudy, and rough land draws down
into an abstract sea its arranged star.

Strange how it's like a dream when two waves past,
and the engine's hum puts villages out of mind
or shakes them together in a waving fashion.
The lights stream northward down a wolfish wind.
A pacing passenger wears the air of one
whom tender arms and fleshly hands embraced.

It's the island that goes away, not we who leave it.
Like an unbearable thought it sinks beyond
assiduous reasoning light and wringing hands,
or, as a flower roots deep into the ground,
it works its darkness into the gay winds
that blow about us in a later spirit.

RETURNING EXILE

Home he came after Canada
where for many years he drank
his failure into the ground.
Westward lay Lewis. He never wrote.
The snow needs a gay pen.
However at the age of fifty-five
he put on his hat, his painted tie,
and packed his trunk (being just alive).
Quietly he sailed over waters
which made him cry secretly by rails
through which he saw his home all green
and salmon leaping between deer's horns.
Arrived home he attended church
(the watch chain snaking his waistcoat).
None was as black or stiff as he.
He cast his bottles into outer darkness
where someone gnashed his teeth
each evening by the quay
watching the great ship sail out
with the girls laughing
the crew in white
and the bar mazy with mirrors.

Some called her SS Remorse
others the bad ship Envy.

SHE TEACHES *LEAR*

Much to have given up? Martyr, one says?
And to read *Lear* to these condemning ones
in their striped scarves and ties but, in the heart,
tall, cool and definite. Naval, in this art.
'Brought it on himself. He ran away,
then strained to keep his pomp and circumstance.'

Of course it's true. Much to be said for Regan,
Goneril too. Cordelia just a tune,
and also beautiful as I am not.
'Life must be lived. Life is beyond thought.
These two were living.' Who says that? It's Brown.
The smallest one (with glasses) in the room.

So I go home towards his bitterness,
achieved selfishness, clinging so with claws
to chair and pipe, a dreadful bitter man.
He hates all life, yet lives. Helpless in pain,
trains pain on others. 'Pray,' at night he says,
'undo this button', and yet hates, for this,

me out of helplessness. And yet I stay.
'Regan and Goneril had some place to go.'
('Some*where*.' Correct this young American.)
Which side is right? For there is young pale Jean –
she might be one. Responsibility
is weighty, living, in the to-and-fro

of these cool deadly judgments. So she listens,
the true Cordelia, library-white face,
thin-boned and spectacled, speechlessly unhappy

and ready for all art, especially poetry.
'They had some place to go and pure passions.
The rest's hypocrisy.' Purity of the race?

No, not as far as that. Simply a lie,
to live and feed with one so selfish grown,
as age is always selfish. The proud two
spur their tall horses into the bright blue
in search of lust, are willing so to die,
the absolute hunters, Goneril and Regan,

beautiful too with their own spare beauty
when one forgets the haunted piteous fox
(there's always a fox whenever such ride by).
Does Jean, as I do, sniff it? Memory
of dear addictive fences, of the high
tall splendid brutes, past little dreaming flocks.

And yet... More simply: They are what they are,
I am what I am? The sensitive eye
broods by packed windows of interior pain
fastened to writhings, knowing rages mean
often unhappiness, that old men wear
their stubborn angers out of dignity

the failing vigour – eyes, arms, knees.
Gravity pulls them down into the ground.
Last angers blossom on its final lip.
'Lear is a child,' I hear. Is this the deep
Greek brilliant irony? I find my peace
in this dictator because I have no kind

child to nourish? No, it's not quite that.
'We'll come to this,' I cry. 'No,' Moira says,
quite definite and calm. 'If I should come
to such a state, let all drive me from home.'
Easy enough, I think (but hold the thought)
to speak such words when interested praise

makes your face happy at the Saturday
school-club dance, in yellow, and a hand
glides down your bare arm, it seems, forever.
Why should I speak this loud, my own fever?
And then I know it's right as far's mind may
(without sly falsity) hope to understand.

'It's just in case,' I say, 'in case, malformed' –
(how vulnerable ties and scarves, how pure!)
'by living we are made. It's just in case' –
the need, the need! – Polite and curious
they know of no such need (but Jean). Not armed
nor yet disarmed they sit. Sure or unsure

it hasn't touched them yet, the fear of age.
Regan and Goneril seem more natural.
From our own weakness only are we kind.
Admire such ones but know in your own mind
how they would bring upon us innocent carnage,
the end of Lear, and *Lear,* their own worse will.

HAMLET

Sick of the place, he turned him towards night.
The mirrors flashed distorted images
of himself in court dress, with big bulbous eyes,
and curtains swaying in a greenish light.

Save me from these, he cried, I could not kill.
I did not have the true and pure belief
even to marry, reproduce myself
in finite mirrors, tall and visible.

Bad jokes and speeches, I endured them all,
so therefore let my death be a bad joke.
I see in the warped mirrors rapiers shake
their subtle poisons perfuming the hall

reflecting accidents, a circus merely,
a place of mirrors, an absurd conclusion.
Images bounce madly against reason
as, in a spoon, wide pictures, fat and jolly.

I could not kill, but let them have their deaths
imprisoned in this air in which they perish
where only lies and ponderous jokes can flourish

Remove the mirror, for there is no breath.

AT THE SALE

Old beds, old chairs, old mattresses, old books,
old pictures of coiffed women, hatted men,
ministers with clamped lips and flowing beards,
a Duke in his Highland den,
and, scattered among these, old copper fire-guards,
stone water-bottles, stoves and shepherds' crooks.

How much goes out of fashion and how soon!
The double-columned leather-covered tomes
recall those praying Covenanters still
adamant against Rome's
adamant empire. Every article
is soaked in time and dust and sweat and rust. What tune

warbled from that phonograph? Who played
that gap-toothed dumb piano? Who once moved
with that white chamber pot through an ancient room?
And who was it that loved
to see her own reflection in the gloom
of that webbed mirror? And who was it that prayed

holding that Bible in her fading hands?
The auctioneer's quick eyes swoop on a glance,
a half-seen movement. In the inner ring
a boy in serious stance
holds up a fan, a piece of curtaining,
an hour-glass with its trickle of old sand.

We walk around and find an old machine.
On one side pump, on another turn a wheel.
But nothing happens. What's this object for?

Imagine how we will
endlessly pump and turn for forty years
and then receive a pension, smart and clean,

climbing a dais to such loud applause
as shakes the hall for toiling without fail
at this strange nameless gadget, pumping, turning,
each day oiling the wheel
with zeal and eagerness and freshness burning
in a happy country of anonymous laws,

while the ghostly hands are clapping and the chairs
grow older as we look, the pictures fade,
the stone is changed to rubber, and the wheel
elaborates its rayed
brilliance and complexity and we feel
the spade become a scoop, cropping the grass,

and the flesh itself becomes unnecessary.
O hold me, love, in this appalling place.
Let your hand stay me by this mattress here
and this tall ruined glass,
by this dismembered radio, this queer
machine that waits and has no history.

'WHAT'S YOUR SUCCESS?'

What's your Success to me who read the great dead,
whose marble faces, consistent overhead,

outstare my verse? What are your chains to me,
your baubles and your rings? That scrutiny

turns on me always. Over terraced houses
these satellites rotate and in deep spaces

the hammered poetry of Dante turns
light as a wristwatch, bright as a thousand suns.

‘CHILDREN, FOLLOW THE DWARFS’

Children, follow the dwarfs and the giants and the wolves,
into the Wood of Unknowing, into the leaves

where the terrible granny perches and sings to herself
past the tumultuous seasons high on her shelf.

Do not go with the Man with the Smiling Face,
nor yet with the Lady with the Flowery Dress.

Avoid the Crystal, run where the waters go
and follow them past the Icebergs and the Snow.

Avoid the Man with the Book, the Speech Machine,
and the Rinsoed Boy who is forever clean.

Keep clear of the Scholar and the domestic Dog
and, rather than Sunny Smoothness, choose the Fog.

Follow your love, the butterfly, where it spins
over the wall, the hedge, the road, the fence,

and love the Disordered Man who sings like a river
whose form is Love, whose country is Forever.

RETURN TO THE COUNCIL HOUSE

Box on box, on ledge after ledge rising
I used at midnight to come home
to your uniform sparkle on a bare hill,
my Rome of the clamped mussels.

O Rome, city of the wolves,
in what office did a man sit
among diminished clarities
designing you with a rigid appetite?

Under crown after crown of neon light
I approached you, the Yale in my hand,
as to an alien island
whirling in the blue sky of TV

and the wife hoarding her plot
her little handkerchief of green,
where the mower lay on its side
and she had her day for the washing.

From the scarred bus shelter I climbed
to my Rome of fixed lines.
The pad of the wolves is tense
among the chequered shadows,

the drift of figures in the blue caves,
the writing on the wall,
the stone steps in their spiral,
from room to room the same.

DUNCAN BAN MACINTYRE

This Gaelic bard fell in love with a small corrie.
Patiently he numbered each blade of grass
with an attentiveness akin to fury
or Celtic monk carving a Celtic cross
with such an intent delicacy, such precision,
that love itself made visionary what was
merely a little corrie. Without passion
it would have remained what now it no longer is.

Now it's more than a corrie. Genius made it
a book, a poem, a place to be wondered at.
Strange deer move in it. It is green-shaded
with a peculiar unalterable light.
A remarkable place soaked in the spirit of one
who was gentle happy tranquil and a careful
meticulous poet who loved every stone
and every slope, and who was always cheerful.

Who knew the way the sun settled just there
at a certain time of day and how that shadow
seemed to vibrate in the evening air.
And the deer grazed like cattle in a meadow.
How the hinds and delicate fawns are shy and fearful
and run like pure wind among the shadows and stones,
drinking the air with delicate nostrils. How tearful
on the other hand they die in the sound of guns.

All poetry's made by love and his life shows it.
An ordinary man unable to read or write,
this corrie in Argyllshire made him a poet.
Whatever it was that made that glen all light
worked in his heart till speech was necessary.
Natural as a lark he sang his song
and patient too as a scientist who would marry
music to fact, research to a musical tongue.

from HOMAGE TO GEORGE ORWELL

I

You knew well in advance
of the rest of us what's true –
that you can't look at a rose
without seeing a Fascist
with his closed red fist.
That the hazy hills
around us every day
are the hills of Spain
where the dry olives
patter into graves.
That 'concentration' means,
among other things,
concentration camps.
And that over the leaves
of your loose notebook
not the light of the lamp
only, but the two
yellow eyes of the sick
Deutschland, the paranoic
warmly-feathered gauleiter,
burning brighter and brighter
nightly on your cottage
implacably perpend.

2

In my little house
on a distant island
I used to scribble poems
on an oil-skinned table.
But I didn't know
what I've learnt to know –
what inhuman pressures
keep a line of verse
on its own course.
How a cult of slaves
kept in their fixed place
the elaborated lines
of a Greek vase.

I BUILD AN ORANGE CHURCH

I build an orange church and put inside it
a little orange minister in a pulpit
that's dandelion yellow.

I make a ceiling of intensest blue.
The seats are heliotrope, the bibles pink,
hymn books are apple green.

Picasso paints the walls with animals.
The angels swoop in red and there's a sun
of blinding nuclear light.

And so transform it all... But for the guilt
that's small and black and creeps in when the door
swings on its oiled hinges.

OLD WOMAN WITH FLOWERS

These are your flowers. They were given to you
so nurse them carefully and tenderly.
Though flowers grow freely elsewhere, here in this room
there's not much space, so therefore like a child
let no one else go near them.
                                        O dear God
wherever you are, I am almost driven wild
by your frightening flowers whose blossoms are turned to bone
for an old woman to look at, in a small room alone.

from WORLD WAR ONE

They droop out of the twilight, slack-rifled,
their eyes tired to stone, their bayonets green.
Around them, an insane loom of light.

A letter winks from a cold pocket.
'Dear Son,' 'Dear Bill.' (A house made of bone
furrows an unmitigated distance.)

Laces trail. This is a sky of heroes
where the small birds are too awed to sing.
Kettles boil in the depths of heads.

Sleepwalking, they pass our tall statues.
Poppies fall on their heads. They don't halt.
They march under the foam of speeches.

As if they're tired. As if they don't see.
Nevertheless their eyes are open.
Strangely in the noise one fixes bayonet,

charges. The blade sinks in wreaths.
He screams onward like a train
through the green pastures of England.

HEAR US, O LORD

Hear us, O Lord. Aggression is part of us.
You polish your jewellery in the salons of heaven.
Everything about you glitters, your wristwatch, the diamond
at your invisible breast, below your invisible beard.

We are such ferocious animals, Lord, we're irrational.
The long journey of the lizard was propelled by this
to the green Jaguar standing in the driveway.
As you polish your nails, we begin to hate you.

All those who tell us the truth we hate.
All those who were strong – like Hitler and Stalin – we loved.
We are obsessed by the table with the green light on it.
We practise with knives in the boudoir and the church.

Ah, if it were only a game. But all things happen.
Because we have spoken too much, a heaven has fallen.
Because we have loved too much, a door has been slammed.
We stare at the light of Envy, green in the night.

What should we do to be saved? The screen slowly brightens.
You watch us with interest, a glass of pale wine in your hand.

'The things that they do, the plays that my actors perform.'

We keep you alive in the silence, in an absence of angels.

SHALL GAELIC DIE?

(translated by the author)

1

A picture has no grammar. It has neither evil nor good. It has only colour, say orange or mauve.
Can Picasso change a minister? Did he make a sermon to a bull?
Did heaven rise from his brush? Who saw a church that is orange?
In a world like a picture, a world without language, would your mind go astray, lost among objects?

2

Advertisements in neon, lighting and going out, 'Shall it... shall it... Shall Gaelic... shall it... shall Gaelic... die?'

3

Words rise out of the country. They are around us. In every month in the year we are surrounded by words.
Spring has its own dictionary, its leaves are turning in the sharp wind of March, which opens the shops.
Autumn has its own dictionary, the brown words lying on the bottom of the loch, asleep for a season.
Winter has its own dictionary, the words are a blizzard building a tower of Babel. Its grammar is like snow.
Between the words the wild-cat looks sharply across a No-Man's-Land, artillery of the Imagination.

4

They built a house with stones. They put windows in the house, and doors. They filled the room with furniture and the beards of thistles.
They looked out of the house on a Highland world, the flowers, the glens, distant Glasgow on fire.
They built a barometer of history.
Inch after inch, they suffered the stings of suffering.
Strangers entered the house, and they left.
But now, who is looking out with an altered gaze? What does he see?
What has he got in his hand? A string of words.

5

He who loses his language loses his world. The Highlander who loses his language loses his world.
The space ship that goes astray among planets loses the world.
In an orange world how would you know orange? In a world without evil how would you know good?
Wittgenstein is in the middle of his world. He is like a spider.
The flies come to him. 'Cuan' and 'coill' rising.
When Wittgenstein dies, his world dies.
The thistle bends to the earth. The earth is tired of it.

6

I came with a 'sobhrach' in my mouth. He came with a 'primrose.'

'A primrose by the river's brim.' Between the two languages,
the word 'sobhrach' turned to 'primrose'.
Behind the two words, a Roman said 'prima rosa'.
The 'sobhrach' or the 'primrose' was in our hands. Its reasons
belonged to us.

7

'That thing about which you cannot speak, be silent about it.'
Was there a pianist before a piano? Did Plato have a
melodeon? Melodeon in the heavens? Feet dancing in the
heavens? Red lips and black hair? Was there a melodeon in
the heavens? A skeleton of notes.

8

'Shall Gaelic die?' A hundred years from now who will say
these words?
Who will say, 'Co their'? Who? The voice of the owl.

9

If I say 'an orange church' will I build an orange church?
If I say 'a mauve minister' will I create him?
The tartan is in its own country.
The tartan is a language.
A Campbell is different from a Macdonald (this is what a
tartan teaches).
The tartans fight each other. Is that why they had to put a
colourless church between them?

10

Said Alexander Macdonald, 'It was Gaelic that Adam and Eve spoke in that garden.' Did God speak Gaelic as well, when he told them about the apple? And when they left that garden, were they like exiles sailing to… Canada?

11

Shall Gaelic die? What that means is: shall we die?

12

An orange church with green walls. A picture on a wall showing ships like triangles. On another wall, a picture of a café with men made of paint. 'Gloria Deo' in the language of paintings, an orange bell, a yellow halo around the pulpit where there are red dancers.

13

Were you ever in a maze? Its language fits your language. Its roads fit the roads of your head. If you cannot get out of the language you cannot get out of the maze. Its roads reflect your language.
O for a higher language, like a hawk in the sky, that can see the roads, that can see their end, like God who built the roads, our General Wade.
The roads of the Highlands fit the roads of our language.

14

When the ape descended from the trees he changed his language. He put away the green leaves. He made small sharp words, words made of stones.

15

The dove returned to Noah with a word in his mouth.

16

The scholar is sitting with a candle in front of him. He is construing words. He is building a dictionary. Little by little, inch by inch, he is building a dictionary. Outside the window the children are shouting, a ball is rising to the sky, a girl and a boy are walking without language to bed. What will he do when the ball enters the quiet room, breaking the window, stopping him at B, and Z so distant.

17

Whom have you got in the net? Who is rising with green eyes, with a helmet, who is in the net?
Cuchulain is in the net, he is rising from the sea, ropes of moonlight at his heels, ropes of language.

18

'When you turn your back on the door, does the door exist?'
said Berkeley, the Irishman who was alive in the soul.
When the Highlands loses its language, will there be a
Highlands, said I, with my two coats, losing, perhaps, the
two.

19

A million colours are better than one colour, if they are
different.
A million men are better than one man if they are different.
Keep out of the factory, O man, you are not a robot. It wasn't
a factory that
made your language – it made you.

20

Like a rainbow, like crayons, spectrum of beautiful languages.
The one-language descended like a church – like a blanket,
like mist.

21

God is outside language, standing on a perch. He crows
now and again. Who hears him? If there is a God let him
emanate from the language, a perfume emanating from the
dew of the morning, from the various-coloured flowers.

22

Death is outside the language. The end of language is beyond language. Wittgenstein didn't speak after his death. What language would he speak? In what language would you say, 'Fhuair a' Ghaidhlig bas?'

23

When the name 'Adam' was called, he turned his back on the hills. He saw his shadow at his feet – he drew his breath.

24

You cannot say, 'Not-Adam'. You cannot say 'Not-Eve'. The apple has a name as well. It is in the story.

25

The gold is new. It will not rust. 'Immutable universal,' as the Frenchman said. But the pennies, the pounds, the half-crowns, these coins that are old and dirty, the notes that are wrinkled like old faces, they are coping with time,
to these I give my allegiance, to these I owe honour, with sweetness.
'Immutable, perfect,' Midas with his coat of gold and of death.

NOTES

Cuan means 'sea' and *coill* means 'wood'. *Co their?* – 'Who will say?'
Fhuair a' Ghaidhlig bas – 'Gaelic is dead.'

FOR JOHN MACLEAN, HEADMASTER, AND CLASSICAL AND GAELIC SCHOLAR

I

The coloured roses fade along the wall.
How shall we live? How perfectly they fall,
the October leaves in yellow, how exact
the woods appear, so married to the fact
of their own unwilled and accurate funeral
without interrogation. In this tract

the dazzling hearse has led us to, we stand,
hats in our hands. The serious piper plays
'The Lament for the Children' and we hear the bound
and ribboned bouquets thudding. Then we take our ways
to the waiting cars across unechoing ground

or over crackling gravel. It remains,
the body in the casket, and begins
its simple mineral weathering. We return
to our complex human burning. What we mourn
changes as we mourn it, and routines
wed and enring us as we move and burn.

II

For you it was the case that Homer lived
in our fluorescence, that Ulysses homed
through our stained and plaguey light, that Hector grieved
in his puncturable armour, that engraved
even in Skye was marble which consumed
the bodies of live Greeks who shaped and carved

contemporary sculpture. Under leaves
which dappled your warm garden (as the groves
of autumnal classic Greece) you turned a page
or made an emendation in a passage.
Exactitude's a virtue, so believes
the inveterate scholar. Happy who can judge

evil as a hiatus or a false
quantity in harmony, who knows
that what protects us from the animals
is language healthy as a healthy pulse
and that our moral being can like prose
be manifestly tested where it fails.

III

I know that it is waning, that clear light
that shone on all our books and made them white
with unanswerable grammar. That the slaves
sustained our libraries and that the wolves
and watchful eagles nourished an elite
and that the elegant and forceful proofs

of their geometers will not suffice.
I know that Athene is wandering now,
dishevelled in the shrubbery, and the nurse
beckons at evening to her. Gods rehearse
their ruined postures and the ruined brow
reflects from mirrors not of fire but ice

and that our brute Achilles drives his wheels
across the gesturing shadows: and that kneels
to cheering legions Aphrodite: packs

are watching Ajax hacking with his axe
inanely the pale sheep: and shady deals
illuminate Odysseus's tracks.

IV

You were a teacher also: what we've learned
is also what we teach: and what we are
cannot be hidden, though we walk black-gowned
along the radiant corridors, profound
in serious scholarship and that precious star
proposed by art or conscience. Where you burned

exactitude prevailed, the rule of Rome,
the gravitas of Brutus and his calm,
his stoic tenderness, his love of books,
his principles and practice. For the Dux
stands in his place, the overwhelming psalm
enchants him wholly among clean-limbed Greeks,

and if you touch him he gives out true coin.
Echo on echo, pupils make a world
which is their bronze and yours, and they will join
link on bright link to make the legions shine
with ethics and with elegance. The absurd
becomes a simple weather, clear and fine.

V

The October leaves are falling. None condemns
their seasonal abdication. What consumes
their crowns and robes is natural, a law

that's common to the weasel and the crow.
They hear no music of the funeral drums
and no cortèges shade the way they go,

no mountains brood, nor does the sharp wind mourn
nor tragic clouds move slowly. For the ice
steadily thickens over lake and corn.
In this pure azure there's no paradise
nor the hell nor purgatory that we devise
lest in the world we shiver and we burn

without the falcon's unhistorical aim,
its brutal beak, the momentary tomb
of its spontaneous moments. Or the sheep
that grazes in its own forgetful sleep
or the barbarians that struck at Rome,
its pompous destiny and shadowed hope.

VI

Though it is finished now, that scholarship,
though vases crack and hourly we may graze
on superficial quanta: though we sleep
abandoned to disorder, and the days
are flashes of small light: and what we praise
is transient and odd, we yet may keep

pictures of autumn, graver, more restrained,
with a finer balance of the weighty mind,
a wind from Rome and Greece which held our course
steady to a harbour where salt oars
received their justice and to scales assigned
the soul would shiver with a stronger force

which now in neon vibrates. But in light
(let it be legend) accompanied the leaves
to their natural assignations and the fruit
bowed to a holy earth. The swan that moves
in reedy waters bows its neck. The waves
receive it, flesh and shadow, day and night.

VII

So with your battered helmet let you be
immersed in golden autumn as each tree
accepts its destiny and will put by
its outworn crown, its varying finery,
and let the humming of the latest bee
bear its last honey home. Beneath this sky

the hexagonal coffin crowned with flowers restores
your body to the earth from which we came
to build our shaking ladders. What was yours
was no phantasmal order, and your name
planted in this place held to its aim
from wider deeper origins. If there were pyres

then a pyre you should have had, and lictors too.
And phantom legions. In this perfect blue
imagine therefore flame that's amber, yellow,
leaves of good flame, volumes that burn and glow,
the foliage of your autumn, where you grew
and where you are buried in the earth you know.

DEAR HAMLET

Dear Hamlet, you were pushed beyond your strength
you had a white face and black clothes,
you stood at corners listening.

Surrounded by the voices and wondering what you should do.
The old father whom you admired so much
but who had driven you to Wittenberg
lay murdered.

To avenge him when you did not even like him
(though you admired him) wasn't easy.
He had won so many battles but you,
you had won none.

Poor schoolboy, longing to be like your father,
learning to fence when he had used an axe,
learning philosophy because he hadn't done so.
Words are not enough.

Rushing about from one commandment to another
you were finally focussed as a target
by Claudius, the small and simple man,
yes, he was simple.

So little sufficed him, just a queen, a kingdom,
salutes from guards, dinners with dinner-jackets,
bow-ties and crowns, the glitter of cut-glass,
the colour of poison.

But you, you needed more. That more was death.
You chewed it, fed on it, watched for it in mirrors,
hunted the castle for it, loved it the best
of anything you had known.

How silly Fortinbras was, not to see it
standing behind him just as he took the crown.
That was the moment he began to die
and you began to live.

HOW OFTEN I FEEL LIKE YOU

Ah, you Russians, how often I feel like you
full of ennui, hearing the cry of wolves
on frontiers of green glass.
In the evening
one dreams of white birches and of bears.
There are picnics in bright glades and someone talking
endlessly of verse as if mowing grass,
endlessly of philosophy round and round
like a red fair with figures of red soldiers
spinning forever at their 'Present Arms'.
How long it takes for a letter to arrive.
Postmen slog heavily over the steppes
and drop their dynamite through the letter-box.
For something is happening everywhere but here.
Here there are Hamlets and old generals.
Everyone sighs and says 'Ekh' and in the stream
a girl is swimming naked among gnats.
This space is far too much for us like time.
Even the clocks have asthma. There is honey,
herring and ham and an old samovar.
Help us, let something happen, even death.
God has forgotten us. We are like fishers
with leather leggings dreaming in a stream.

from RUSSIAN POEM

I

I am too old for you.
Nevertheless
in summer under a crown of leaves…
I am in debt,
a kind of Hamlet.
Nevertheless,
Sonia, you are beautiful.
I've left my Jewish wife
mooning from piano to vodka.
She coughs all night.
You do not know the guilt…
Here in the sunshine it is fine,
you in your white dress…
People, such people.
Generals
with false red faces
booming like snipes.
Old uncles, aunts,
surplus to requirements.
Sonia,
there was a time
when I had ideals
Now my back is broken.
I feel nothing, Sonia,
even should you put
lightly your hand in mine,
even should you kiss
I'd not awaken.
Sonia, I'm afraid
of this old skin.

II

Ennui covers the land.
Broken fences.
Russia is full of broken fences.
Pigs root in the muck.
Grandfathers roast themselves on stoves.
Ash on their waistcoats.

Something is bound to happen.
They click their heels like toys,
kiss over olives
fine, and cared-for, hands.
There's something I'm hearing.

Great cannon in small ears.
The stone heads tremble.
The wolves trouble our wit.
They are seething like water.

III

Hear us, Philosophy will not save us.
In our salons we have talked the 'soul' to death.

Our cigar smoke snakes from the orchard
where the apples ripen and the small hands

shine.

Our glasses reflect the sunset. Our monocles
have a raw glare. The uncles

twinkle like robins.

We have talked the 'soul' to death. Now as the sun goes down
we shiver and go in.

VI

'We shall soon go to Moscow,' say the sisters
watching the great bear at the edge of the forest
bumbling along, so neat and strong.

There is the taste of autumn in the air,
the taste of aisles and pillars and of lemon,
the taste of tall clear glasses on the lawn.

The bear trots amiably among the steeples.
They watch him through their telescopes so mild,
so cuddly and ingenuous. He stares

back through the telescope. And the trees shake.
The glasses shake, the ringless pale hands,
and Moscow in their silk sways without sound.

X

Sonia, my fine ghost,
I see you among the rifles.
You were saying 'What need of a psychiatrist?
He would only stare at my wrist.'

Sonia, you were a sign of the times
a young girl vibrating out of phase.
I see you wearing white slacks,
legs spread apart,
reading old leaves.

Sonia, you were a generator
bouncing on a piece of waste ground.

Sonia, it has come at last.
The newspapers have gone mad.
They are punching out Reality.

If I do not die now I shall die.

Sonia, I stretch out my hand to you.
I am afraid but I stretch out my hand to you.
Sonia, let us follow the wind.

FOR KEATS

Genius is so strange,
you were in so many ways ordinary
in so many ways wounded like us.

But the vase beckons –
continually the vase beckons –
the imperfect bird sings
in the brown mortal leaves.

Poor Tom dies in the white linen.
Sore throats! Do nightingales have sore throats?
In the nightingale's pure notes
what eloquent disease?

Happily to seek the classic –
that land without fatigue –
that which stands like the rocks of Staffa
black remarkable architecture of the sea
solider than weeping Skye.

Than the grass of summer,
devotees of England's spas,
the irritabilities of the second rate,
the helmet bruised and vain.

Fighting the scree, to arrive at Autumn,
innocent impersonal accepted
where the trees do not weep like gods
but are at last themselves.

Bristly autumn, posthumous and still,
the crowning fine frost on the hill
the perfect picture blue and open-eyed
with the lakes as fixed as your brother's eyes,
autumn that will return

and will return and will return, however
the different delicate vase revolves
in the brown mortal foliage, in the woods
of egos white as flowers.

GAELIC SONGS

I listen to these songs
from a city studio.
They belong to a different country,
to a barer sky,
to a district of heather and stone.
They belong to the sailors
who kept their course
through nostalgia and moonlight.
They belong to the maidens
who carried the milk in pails
home in the twilight.
They belong to the barking of dogs,
to the midnight of stars,
to the sea's terrible force,
exile past the equator.
They belong to the sparse grass,
to the wrinkled faces,
to the houses sunk in the valleys,
to the mirrors
brought home from the fishing.

Now they are made of crystal
taking just a moment
between two programmes
elbowing them fiercely
between two darknesses.

IN THE CHINESE RESTAURANT

Because we'd never go there, it was good,
those years together. We'd never need to go
though we could talk of it and so we were
happy together in a place we'd made
so small and airless that we couldn't leave.
But we could think of it and say, 'Perhaps
we'll go there someday.' But we could not go
for as we lived so we'd lost all the maps.
It grew more perfect as the slow years passed
as if we were there already. One fine day
we'd find it all around us if we looked.
We would be in it, even old and grey.

So that, one night, in that late restaurant
with Chinese waiters round us we picked up
the menu in Chinese and understood
every single word of it. It was
a revelation when the waiters smiled.
They looked so clear as the glasses slowly filled.

GIVE ME YOUR HAND

Give me your hand.
Do you not feel it,
the first chill of autumn?
The azure is razor sharp
the brown nostalgic.

There is no noise.
The light is single
under the uncrowned trees
It is beaten like steel
interrupted by litter.

Ah, the queens are all gone
with their brocade and silken
garments of the summer.
Without their fripperies
they are naked like us.

We are at zero.
There is no babbling
of water over stones.
The stones are bearded
with unshaken moss.

The trees are thermometers
almost transparent.
There is no sap
or it's descended
to an absent country.

Give me your hand,
we are two orphans
with large blue eyes
in a story of Andersen's
on an autumnal journey.

CHRISTMAS, 1971

There's no snow this Christmas... there was snow
when we received the small horses and small cart,
brothers together all those years ago.
There were small watches made of liquorice
surrealist as time hung over chairs.
I think perhaps that when we left the door
of the white cottage with its fraudulent icing
we were quite fixed as to our different ways.
Someone is waving with black liquorice hands
at the squashed windows as the soundless bells
and the soundless whips lash our dwarf horses forward.
We diverge at the road-end in the whirling snow
never to meet but singing, pulling gloves
over and over our disappearing hands.

IN THE TIME OF THE USELESS PITY

In the time of the useless pity I turned away
from your luminous clock-face in the hopeless dark,
appealing to me greenly, appealing whitely.
Nothing I could do, I had tried everything,
lain flat on the rug, fluttered my spaniel paws,
offered you my house like an unlocked crystal –
and so it came, the time of the useless pity
when the roots had had enough of you, when they slept,
elaborating themselves by themselves
when they shifted over from yours, seeking a place
different from yours to burst through and to pierce
with a royal purple, straight and delicate: sails
of the suave petals unfurling at the mast.

EVERYTHING IS SILENT

Everything is silent now
before the storm.
The transparent walls tremble.
You can hear the very slightest hum
of a stream miles away.

The silence educates your ear.
The threat is palpable.
You can hear the boots beyond the mountains.
You can hear the breathings of feathers.
You can hear the well of your heart.

You know what it is that permits the walls,
that allows the ceiling,
that lets the skin cling to your body,
that mounts the spiral
of your beholden bones.

That sorrow is a great sorrow
and leaves you radiant
when the tempest has passed
and your vases are still standing
and your bones are stalks in the water.

THIS GOODBYE

This goodbye
was the closing of two doors,
the dimming of two circles.

This goodbye
was not an assembling of
precious souvenirs.

This goodbye
happened so quickly I
was not aware of it.

It was just that I was not looked at.
It was just
an injustice of the glass.

'YOU TOLD ME ONCE'

You told me once how your younger brother died.
It was by drowning. In the tar-black sea
he sang a psalm to bring his rescuers near.
That did not save him though. One cannot hide,
you would have said, from destiny. So here
there are two meanings working side by side.

You died of lack of oxygen. I tried
to fit the mask against your restless face
in the bumpy ambulance in which you lay.
I thought that moment of the psalm as guide
beyond our vain technology, the grey
and scarlet blankets that you tossed aside.

ON LOOKING AT THE DEAD

This is a coming to reality.
This is the stubborn place. No metaphors swarm

around that fact, around that strangest thing,
that being that was and now no longer is.

This is a coming to a rock in space
worse than a rock (or less), diminished thing

worse and more empty than an empty vase.

The devious mind elaborates its rays.
This is the stubborn thing. It will not move.

It will not travel from our stony gaze.

But it must stay and that's the worst of it
till changed by processes. Otherwise it stays.

To beat against it and no waves of grace
ever to ascend or sovereign price

to be held above it! This is no hero. This
is an ordinary death. If there is grace

theology is distant. Sanctify
(or so they say) whatever really is

and this is real, nothing more real than this.
It beats you down to it, will not permit

the play of imagery, the peacock dance,
the bridal energy or mushrooming crown

or any blossom. It only is itself.
It isn't you. It only is itself.

It is the stubbornness of a real thing

mentionable as such and only such,
the eyes returning nothing. Compromise

is not a meaning of this universe.
And that is good. To face it where it is,

to stand against it in no middle way
but in the very centre where things are

and having it as centre, for you take
directions from it not as from a book

but from this star, black and fixed and here,
a brutal thing where no chimeras are

nor purple colours nor a gleam of silk
nor any embroideries eastern or the rest

but unavoidable beyond your choice
and therefore central and of major price.

‘OF THE UNCOMPLICATED DAIRY GIRL’

Of the uncomplicated dairy girl
in gown that’s striped in blue and red
feeding the hens in a windy spring
by the green wooden shed
where shade after quick shade
endlessly shuttles let me speak
and speak unsorrowing.

As in the weather of a Lewis loom
a pastoral picture, striped against the blue,
against the stone, against the green,
against the cottage with its daisies
taking the place of roses
casting the meal from a young hand
still without its ring.

The long dress billows in the breeze
mixed like the confectionery
you’d bring home from the fishing
in the large yellow chest with hats,
silken things and coats,
just before your straight-backed brother
marched off to save the King.

Just stay there therefore for a moment,
uncomplicated dairy girl,
in your chequered screen of red and blue
holding the pail in your hand
before the sky is red and mooned
and feathered by (beyond the dance)
the beat of metal wings.

AT THE SCOTT EXHIBITION, EDINBURGH FESTIVAL

I

He will outlast us, churning out his books,
advocate and historian, his prose
earning him Abbotsford with its borrowed gates,
its cheap mementos from the land he made.
Walking the room together in this merciless
galaxy of manuscripts and notes
I am exhausted by such energy.
I hold your hand for guidance. Over your brow
the green light falls from tall and narrow windows.
His style is ignorant of this tenderness,
the vulnerable angle of your body
below the Raeburn with its steady gaze.

II

It was all in his life, not in his books
'Oh I am dying, take me home to Scotland
where I can breathe though that breath were my last.'
He limped through an Edinburgh being made anew.
He worked his way through debts, past a dead wife.
My dear, we love each other in our weakness
as he with white grave face diminishing through
stroke after stroke down to the unpaid room.
We know what we are but know not what we will be.
I tremble in this factory of books.
What love he must have lost to write so much.

from *Penguin Modern Poets 21* (1972)

JEAN BRODIE'S CHILDREN

Jean Brodie's children in your small green caps,
I hear you twitter down the avenues.

The great round bells ring out, the Mademoiselle
despairs of English. In the rustling dorms
you giggle under sheets.

'Dear Edinburgh, how I remember you,
your winter cakes and tea, your bright red fire,
your swirling cloaks and clouds.

Your grammar and your Greek, the hush of leaves,
No Orchids for Miss Blandish with a torch
beneath the tweedy blanket.

Ah, those beautiful days, all green and shady,
our black and pleated skirts, our woollen stockings,
our ties of a calm mauve.

Mistresses, iron in their certainty,
their language unambiguous but their lives
trembling on grey boughs.'

IF YOU ARE ABOUT TO DIE NOW

If you are about to die now
there is nothing I can write for you.
History is silent about this.
Even Napoleon, face huge as a plate,
disguised the advance guard and said:
'Why they sent for my brother is because
he, and not I, is in trouble.'

The screens come down. The nurses disappear
like the tails of fishes. The clouds
are white as cotton wool and also
Dettol outlives the perfume.
The unshaven man in the next ward
is given shaving lotion for Christmas.
Sorrow stands like a stork on one leg,
brooding.

The coloured windows give way to plain.
The horsemen crossing the moor are comrades
going the other way into the country
of the undisciplined and the free.
Here there is the Land of the Straight Lines
with a banner black and silent,
a black mirror
with the image of an old rose.

History does not warn us of this.
Napoleon's face expands to a window.
The manic thoughts fly outwards, beating.
'The documents did not tell me.
There was no announcement in the salon.
Why is it that the chairs are getting crooked?
Why is it that my army does not hear me?
They are eating, laughing by the stream.

I shout to them, "Put on your armour."
But they do not listen.
They do not know me, they are relapsing
into the marsh of their idleness.
They are schoolboys escaped from Latin.
O how afraid they are of Excellence.
They admire their faces in the water.

They splash in the new bubbles.'

from THE WHITE AIR OF MARCH

I

This is the land God gave to Andy Stewart –
we have our inheritance.
There shall be no ardour, there shall be indifference.
There shall not be excellence, there shall be the average.
We shall be the intrepid hunters of golf balls.

Have you not known, have you not heard, has it not been reported
that Mrs Macdonald has given an hour-long lecture on Islay
and at the conclusion was presented with a bouquet of flowers
by Marjory, aged five?
Have you not noted
the photograph of the whist drive, skeleton hands,
rings on skeleton fingers?
Have you not seen
the glossy weddings in the glossy pages,
champagne and a 'shared joke'.
Do you not see
the Music Hall's still alive here in the North? and on the stage
the yellow gorse is growing.
'Tragedy,' said Walpole, 'for those who feel.
For those who think, it's comic.'
Pity then those who feel
and, as for the Scottish Soldier, off to the wars!
The Cuillins stand and will forever stand.
Their streams scream in the moonlight.

from ORPHEUS

I

And he said, I am come in search of her
bringing my single bitter gift. I have
nothing more precious to offer
than this salt venom seeming to you as love.
It is true I cannot live without her
since I am now shade who was once fire.
See, mineral spirit, how I now suffer
by the slow heavy motion of my lyre.

And the god then replying, Let her stay
for by her absence your music is more clear
barer and purer. Always in the air
her distance will perfect her as Idea.
Better the far sun of an April day
than fleshly thunder in the atmosphere.

2

And he said, That is great condemnation,
to live profoundly and yet much alone.
To see deeply by a barren passion.
It was forgetfully I moved the stone
which now submits to my examination.
She was my sense; around her flowing gown
my poems gathered in their proper season.
They were her harvest yet they were my own.

And the god then replying, What you say
is what her absence taught you. Our return

is not permissible to an earlier way.
If it were possible you would learn to mourn
even more deeply. Do you never burn
poems whose language was becoming grey?

3

And he to the god, If you should let her go
I'd know my music had its former power
to melt you too as once it melted snow
to alter you as once it altered her
so that in music we both learned to grow.
It was a dance of earth and of the air.
But up above it's easier. Here below –
The shade then smiled and said, Behold her there,

and he beheld her whitely where she stood
in that deep shade. She seemed not to have changed
nor he to have changed either as he played.
And yet her apparition was so strange.
She didn't fit the music that he made.
The notes and she were mutually disarranged.

4

And the god to him, Now I must tell you clear
what you refuse to see, since it is hard
to accuse ourselves of cruelty and fear.
You wished that she should die. And what you heard
was not my voice but yours condemning her.
If you will learn to love you must go forward.
For that is how it is in the upper air.
All that you have shared you have now shared.

And Orpheus took his lyre and left that place
and moved where the shadows moved and the clouds flowed
and all that lived had its own changing grace.
As on an April day there was sun and shade
but nothing vicious or virtuous
haunted the various music that he played.

EIGHT SONGS FOR A NEW CEILIDH

Translated from the author's own Gaelic

I

You asked me for a poem for yourself, thinking, I suppose, that I would put you among the stars for beauty and intelligence.

But as for me I grew up in bare Lewis without tree or branch and for that reason my mind is harder than the foolish babble of the heavens, and also at Hiroshima the kettle boiled over our music and in Belsen there was seen an example of dishonour eating love and flesh, and because of that and because of the truth and all the Evil that was done to us, and we ourselves did (among our complaints) I will never put a pen again into my fist for beauty or for intellect. Beauty is dangerous enough and as for the mind did it not spoil the glittering cities of Europe? But when one night I shall hear the quarrelsome beasts of love I will make a song for you that will illuminate the murder of the deer in the heather.*

2

When she took the great sea on her, Lewis went away and will not return. I was not compelled to sail 'over to Australia' but around me is Hiroshima and Pasternak's book is in my hands –

I will not drink a health-giving drink from the spring of the healthy deer of May but from water full of eels which are electric and shivering on my flesh like Venus breaking through the mind and the dark-green of the clouds but it was the fine bareness of Lewis that made the work of my mind like a loom full of the music of the miracles and greatness of our time.

---

* This final sentence is in the original version but omitted from the *Collected Poems*.

3

I saw myself in a camp among the Nazis and the wretched Jews. My hand was white with the innocent lamps of Guernica and my cheeks streaming with piteous tears but in one hand there was a hard gun while the gas was writhing like the mist of Lewis over cold rocks.

4

Standing at the edge of the reservoir that was dumb, menacing, with bare water, I saw the live flies hitting the dead flies on the back. The foxglove was heavy about us with summer's perfume and the sky as limpid as the music of a fiddle. In that moment you leaped and went down into the water, and I was frightened that you wouldn't rise and I shouted in spite of the skill of my intelligence but after that I became silent.

5

I will not climb these mountains for what is at the top?

The stars are holding a ceilidh but what can they say that is not in my own dark depth? I will never sail on a ship. My Pacific is in my head and my Columbus praising countries that are far below. The day of my mind is my May and my twittering of birds the quick thoughts that are black and yellow about my skies.

6

I will never go to France, my dear, my dear, though you are young. I am tied to the Highlands. That is where I learnt my wound.

And are we not tied to that as well? A door will open but where will the slavish spirit of man go? I heard the wind blowing to the Greeks at the Pillars of Hercules: our round world is more harmonious than that. O, it is not a word of manliness that I am speaking of but about the guilt that follows me from mountain and moor. My Uist is inside my head and my love like an agonising tether that is yellow and dangerous and beautiful.

7

'Go to London,' they said to me. 'In the great city you will compose music from the bitter hard light of your stomach.' And I was struggling with myself for many years, thinking of those streets, men with penetrating power in their faces, an illuminated glittering taxi flashing on the windows of my intelligence.

But tonight sitting at the fire and the hills between me and the sky and listening to the empty quietness and seeing the deer coming to my call I think of another one who said the truthful words: 'Look straight down through wood and wood. Look in your own heart and write.'

8

Will you go with me, young maiden, over to Japan where our sanity is wasting in that big bomb that fell on town and on mountain?

Not to Uist among the trees or to green Lewis among the heather nor a Farewell to Finnary burning calmly in the strait nor in the hall of Glasgow or Edinburgh and Duncan Ban walking elegantly with a bright gun among the lies that are clouds round our time.

WHEN WE WERE YOUNG

When we were young it would be raining and we throwing stones at the telegraph poles unceasingly.

One horse would be standing against a wall, drenched by the rain, his skin slippery with the grey rain.

When we were young we would be playing football, with the moon in the sky like a football made of gold.

When we were young old women would be telling us, 'Don't do this, do that' for fear of the owl.

When we were young the sky would be empty, and pictures in the book, and the earth green and distant.

When we were young, there would be lies, when we are old the lie is that youth was without stain.

FREUD

Great man from Vienna who opened the mind with a knife keen with sore efficient happy light, and who saw the seas sweating with the bluegreen ghosts of plague, and uncountable riches.

I follow the beasts with a joy that I cannot tell though I should be fishing from dungeon or from prison, as they move on that sea-bottom in the freedom of truth with their great helmets. No one will bring them to shore.*

Cancer took your jaw away. But you were scanning with profundity the bottom of that sea where there are horrifying shadows. Father, mother and daughter fighting entwined together in a Greek play, in a strangling of forests.

The letter that I will not send, the letter that I will not keep, the poetry that my head cannot put together, the history that I would not want anyone to tell of my planets, the star is below in the seaweed of the skies.

Goodbye to the laughter of nature and the seas, goodbye to the salt that will bring tears to thoughts, goodbye to death which opens valuable countries, our rings are early in the weddings of our gifts.

O miracle of the waves and I tirelessly scrutinising you like a gay porpoise leaping in my country, it was you who gave us these new waves – your monument is on the bottom, and the seas are your pulpit.

---

* This last sentence was omitted from the *Collected Poems*.

THE WHITE SWAN*

The white swan is always there, even in the Great War, especially in the Great War, the white swan is swimming, on a river that they will never reach, those who die and those who return, at the far end of what happened to them, the white swan that will never die. With her long white neck, with her curiosity fishing among the canisters for clean water, where a house will be growing and the little children will be running, and the grey lark rising above distant chimneys.

* The title of a Gaelic love song about the First World War.

FOR DERICK THOMSON

1

We were brought up in Bayble together. There are many years since then. There were ghosts at the edge of the dyke and heather on Hol, and the stone round it. And an owl in the wave, and a wind shaking Mary Roderick, and the hen being blown to the moor. At the tips of our fingers was the dream. But the wind took low Bayble away. The boats are coming towards uncultivated soil and the terrifying corn. What is that cloud with the scowl?

What is that cloud on the Muirneag? What is that Bible opening and the leaves with wind and rain on them? What is the shadow that is troubling me? Whence is the thunder of the river? Who put these fish on the park? That eagle is high above my memory. Whence are these winds, Derick?

2

There is a tall mountain, the mountain of poetry, there is a tall mountain, the mountain of life. Which is the more difficult, which is the higher? The white ghosts are waiting.

Their large eyes are laughing, the helmets of Aignish catching us. O my guilts, O my shame, streets of names, row after row of them.

Above the mountain, mocking, is the sun of the spirit, waiting. Above Bayble, above the horizon, above the wells of life.

Above the great lights of the streets, above Homer, Aberdeen, above the white moon of my friends, above the crayon books.

Above the autumn of nuts, and that tall tree that is waiting. Like hens scattered across moorland, those Greeks who taught us life.

3

Bayble and Athens, isn't the compass strange and strict? How locked the lock is! There is a broken door in the glen.

Greek is on the broken door. There is a hawk on a chimney singing and saying: 'You are laid by. But I will open you to the chest.'

O beautiful hawk, O key of fire, teach me your beautiful poetry, your beak as innocent as a child's and as skilful as the work of intelligence.

4

In his beak he lifted Lewis and Bayble. In his beak he lifted me up. I saw Jupiter with its shadow steering heaviness over my sea.

And Mars and Venus going past, all the planets singing with the sweet choir of the thousand lights.

The Mod of the universe so sweet, bitter and sweet, that white choir, and the poet being crowned in the heavens, his face carved like a hawk's and his wings open, star on star.

5

The cuckoo is in the hawk's mouth. The chicken is in the crow's mouth. (The sore wind is in a great hurry.)

I will not put on my silken coat, my summer coat, in the bad weather and my fool's coat in pieces.

This century is throwing enough water at us like that great coloured tall bus that makes holes in the roads.

I will not leap from it, it is going too fast for me, it is putting the earth upside down. It is putting joy and hate on me, and my hair streaming to that wind, and my white face becoming a diamond against elegies and hymns, against the Iolaire and Holm, that song amongst the psalms, against the darkness and the blue and we now in our time with white lights, smooth lights on us, and Stornoway as small as a pin, but a golden hawk in that high sky like God, looking in a mirror.

ON A BEAUTIFUL DAY

From the stone the wildcat is watching the world. The hare shakes like a lily. The hawk and the lark are in the same mirror and the sun shining and the grass growing. The wildcat is drinking champagne over his teeth. The hare is halted, listening with ears like doors. The hawk is sitting on its wings drinking the wind, and the lark singing like a record in a Gaelic cloud.

THE STONE

I will tell you, my dear, the words that the stone told me. The stone has never heard of Lewis or about songs. The stone is a prisoner under the lightning. The lightning is weaving a light around the stone like an old woman who has gone mad.

The stone is inside the prison thinking about darkness, about clouds, about shells, and about other stones.

But at the end it is thinking of itself alone.

And because of that and because of poetry which is weaving a swift light about the stone, this is what the stone said to me on a winter's night or a summer's night far from the moon and the restless sea that will not find sleep again but is walking the world at three o'clock in the morning.

This is what the stone told me: 'I am waiting. The longest river will reach its end. The brightest spirit will reach its conclusion. And at the end of the matter I will rise in front of it and in the middle of the thunder I will be like a king.'

RAVEN

Writing the last words I gave my pen to a raven. 'What have you to say to them? What story is in your heart?'

He looked at me with cold eyes. He put ice on my sight. And then he wrote with permanence: 'Tell them that I will be paying a visit.'

'But our music,' I said to him. 'Our poetry, book after book. O miracle of the northern lights, the imagination of Dante and Homer.'

'I know,' I shouted to him, 'the Odyssey of greatness. They kept you in mind but swallowed you with hope.'

And he threw down the pen. The window was hard with marvellous and strict light and the raven lost in my comfort.

GAELIC STORIES

1

A fisherman in wellingtons
and his sweetheart
and his mother.

2

A story
about an old man
and a seal.

3

A woman
reading a Bible for seven years
waiting for a sailor.

4

A melodeon.
A peat stack.
An owl.

5

A croft.
Two brothers.
A plate with potatoes.

6

A girl from Glasgow
wearing a mini
in church.

7

The sea
and a drifter,
the Golden Rose.

8

A man who was in Australia
coming home
on a wedding night.

9

A romance
between cheese
and milk.

10

Glasgow
in a world of nylons
and of neon.

11

Two women
talking
in a black house.

12

A monster
rising from the sea,
'Will you take tea?'

13

A comedy
in a kitchen
with jerseys.

14

A conversation
between a loaf and
cheese.

15

A conversation
between a wellington
and a herring.

16

A conversation
between fresh butter
and a cup.

17

A conversation
between Yarmouth
and Garrabost.

18

A moon
hard and high
above a marsh.

THE DAYS ARE PASSING

The days are passing,
we are growing old.
What happened to the dancer in the mirror
with the cloudless face?
The twittering of the birds is further away,
drowned by the humming of the razor,
the towel behind the door
is like a ghost.

Ah, world, did you trick us
or was it that we did not rightly understand you
in those young days
when your face was open
reflecting our own faces?

THE TV

1

The sun rises every day
from moving shadows –
on the TV.

2

We did not believe in the existence of Ireland
till we saw it many nights –
on the TV.

3

He knows more about Humphrey Bogart
than he knows about Big Norman –
since he got the TV.

4

Said Plato –
'We are tied in a cave' –
that is, the TV.

5

A girl came into the room
without perfume without expression –
on the TV.

6

At last he lost the world
as Berkeley said –
there was nothing but the TV.

7

He bought *War and Peace*,
I mean Tolstoy,
after seeing it on the TV.

8

When he switched off the TV
the world went out –
he himself went out.

9

His hands did not come back to him
or his eyes
till he put on the TV.

10

A rose in a bowl on the TV set,
the things that are in the world,
the things that are not.

11

He found himself in the story.
He was in the room.
He didn't know where he was.

12

You, my love, are dearer to me
than Softly Softly
than Sportsnight with Coleman.

13

'In locked rooms with iron gates' –
but, my love,
do they have TV?

IN THE GLEN

The stags come down from the hills and he comes over.
I do not want him for his wife says no.
There are a few houses and that's all,
and a mad gossip of an intellectual
who wears red clothes and a proud phantom crown.
I do not want him but I am alone.
He mends the car and breaks the wood for me.
But I do not want him for his wife says no
and we must live in this community,
dependent on each other. We are leaves.
I hear him coming as the stags come down
gently to drink at the pale evening water
steady and large, their antlers faintly shining.
I hear him crunch the gravel. Through the pane
I see his wife's eyes fixed at another pane.
I watch him coming. He has lost his shame.
I am his drug, he says. The intellectual
walks by the river in her splendid dream.
She thinks we're peasants and her mind is cold,
a heron by the river fishing for books
she read at Cambridge centuries ago.
The stags lift up their heads. The door lies open.
I sit here coldly by the trembling fire
from which I'd cast large rabbits on the wall
for my fatherless children sleeping overhead.
He's standing in the doorway. I am waiting.
I hear the drumming hooves. The heron's chased them.
His shadow climbs the wall and he is here.
He is so tall beyond my warm small chair.

MY UNCLE

In '18 the M.O. said:
'You've got six months to live,'
demobbing him among the dead,
issuing him with a civvy shroud,
a kit for the churchyard.

'I'll piss on your grave,' he answered
and strode into the raw
postwar 'twenties, then 'thirties,
almost collapsing America's
green twilight of the hurt cities,

marrying a Scottish 'lass',
growing richer, settling down,
tending his large garden
when the Rising Sun of Japan
parched his adopted nation.

This year at eighty-six
he flies home for a while
to the Scotland that he once left
to fight against old Kaiser Bill,
his melodeon in his case.

Back home he drives a Plymouth Fury.
Here he'd hire a car.
'But all my schoolmates are dead.
It's entertainment to read
the obituary columns.'

'Reading is your life,' he says
shrewdly and then adds,
'We couldn't speak English good
but we got by, goddamit.
We had to, in them days.'

Says, 'At my age you're not afraid
of dying. You just wait.
That goddam M.O.'s dead.'
Like an old craggy laureate
he talks on till midnight.

'I never use them damn pills.
What's happened to this place?
Why does no one ever dance?
Son, I use to be a prince
with my melodeon.'

I see him off on a large plane.
He waves. He will arrive
at midnight in his own house.
Having outlived his wife,
'I'll have to do a few chores.'

The plane climbs. We'll not see
either the other again.
I've bought him an Alistair MacLean.
'I always read books twice, son,'
he says as he turns away.

THE WORKMEN

The workmen sing like birds in the scaffolding
ascending and descending ladders, leaning
against the iron struts in the sunny day.
They're merely boys, bare-armed, their shirts streaming
into the breeze which wanders as at play.
They are like birds at play, their teeth gleaming
whitely as we look up from below.

The struts are branches and the iron poles
they push up to each other are the straws
of a vast iron nest which they are making.
How effortless they are in that high place,
how easily they move and wave, unshaken
by any fear. How casual their grace
though you can hear them swearing, see them mocking

the spectators down below, appalled by height
admiring for the moment the young boys
in dusty trousers, comic acrobats.
The world can see them now in their careless poise
showing off to the business-men in bowler hats,
the girls in summer dresses. Who employs
such natural comics, such ironic cats

thumbing their noses at us while still raising
this complex structure, this vast iron tree
they flit about in, level to dizzy level?
A pilot flying low might later see
their names written in chalk as RANDY NEVILLE
NODDY and GROOVY, an eternity
to be washed out by rain as by the uncivil

upward-looking spectators who will later
forget the builder when the building's done
and are perhaps famishing for their fall.
But the boys will have their glory in the sun
monkeying about and briefly famous while
the air is fresh and warm and breezes run
and the cafes far below are matchbox small.

CHINESE POEM

I

To Seumas Macdonald,
    now resident in Edinburgh –
I am alone here, sacked from the Department
for alcoholic practices and disrespect.
A cold wind blows from Ben Cruachan.
There is nothing here but sheep and large boulders.
Do you remember the nights with *Reliquiae Celticae*
and those odd translations by Calder?
Buzzards rest on the wires. There are many seagulls.
My trousers grow used to the dung.
What news from the frontier? Is Donald still Colonel?
Are there more pupils than teachers in Scotland?
I send you this by a small boy with a pointed head.
Don't trust him. He is a Campbell.

2

The dog brought your letter today
from the red postbox on the stone gate
two miles away and a bit.
I read it carefully with tears in my eyes.
At night the moon is high over Cladach
and the big mansions of prosperous Englishmen.
I drank a half bottle thinking of Meg
and the involved affairs of Scotland.
When shall we two meet again
in thunder, lightning or in rain?
The carrots and turnips are healthy,
the *Farmer's Weekly* garrulous.

Please send me a *Radio Times* and a book
on cracking codes. I have much sorrow.
Mrs Macleod has a blue lion on her pants.
They make a queenly swish in a high wind.

3

There is a man here who has been building a house
for twenty years and a day.
He has a barrow in which he carries large stones.
He wears a canvas jacket.
I think I am going out of my mind.
When shall I see the city again,
its high towers and insurance offices,
its glare of unprincipled glass?
The hens peck at the grain.
The wind brings me pictures of exiles,
ghosts in tackety boots, lies,
adulteries in cornfields and draughty cottages.
I hear Donald is a brigadier now
and that there is fighting on the frontier.
The newspapers arrive late with strange signs on them.
I go out and watch the road.

4

Today I read five books.
I watched Macleod weaving a fence
to keep the eagles from his potatoes.
A dull horse is cobwebbed in rain.
When shall our land consider itself safe
from the assurance of the third rate mind?

We lack I think nervous intelligence.
Tell them I shall serve in any capacity,
a field officer, even a private,
so long as I can see the future
through uncracked field glasses.

5

A woman arrived today
in a brown coat and a brown muff.
She says we are losing the war,
that the Emperor's troops are everywhere
in their blue armour and blue gloves.
She says there are men in a stupor
in the ditches among the marigolds
crying 'Alas, alas.'
I refuse to believe her.
She is, I think, an agent provocateur.
She pretends to breed thistles.

from THE NOTEBOOKS OF ROBINSON CRUSOE

Island, what shall I say of you, your peat bogs, your lochs, your moors and berries?
The cry of your birds in the fading evening.
Your flowers in summer glowing brightly where there are no thoroughfares.
The perpetual sound of the sea.
The spongy moss on which feet imprint themselves.
The mountains which darken and brighten like ideas in the mind.
The owl with its big glasses that perches on a late tree listening.
The mussels clamped to the rocks, the fool's gold, the tidal pools filling and emptying.
The corn that turns from pale green to yellow, my scarecrow rattling in the wind.
The smoke that arises from my fire.

This I say:
One man cannot warm the world.
This I say:
The world of one man is different from the world of many men.

This I say:
Without the net, the sweetest fish are tasteless.

IN THE SURGERY

1

What in this place are they waiting to be cured of?
Headaches, insomnia and the vulgar small
unmentionable odours of the body.
They are reading magazines, their heads bowed.
They turn to the horoscopes and the love stories.
A child with its loving mother gains their attention –
it looks so healthy as if no disease
could get a grip of it or dull its blue eyes.
They are waiting for the receptionist to shout their names.
The question is: what are they suffering from?
Is it death that is fixed in their bodies or a lack of life?

2

The receptionist has said: No dogs permitted.
On Saturdays, Emergency Cases Only.
Don't send for your doctor in the dead of night.
He needs his beauty sleep like other people.
The receptionist wears white like a starched angel.
She's always speaking in the telephone.
Is she happy here, bringing the ill together
in the one room on such a fine day?

3

The doctor says: There's nothing wrong with you
that a hunk of life can't cure.
Meanwhile, I'll give you pills which are red and black.

Take three each day, eat plenty of oranges.
And if you die, why that's nothing.
Plenty of people have died and been buried also.
When you come back we'll start all over.
Meanwhile Good Morning and stop worrying.

4

So I went away and stared into the water.
People were passing by and some were laughing.
They all flowed with the stream in their coloured clothes.
It is true what he said: There's no cure for it.
The new children are taught their alphabet,
and the new mothers enjoy their miracles.
What is in the water but more water?
If you close your eyes, you hear the endless footsteps.

IN SLEEP

Sometimes when I sleep I am among the dead.
They are all laughing and joking.
They walk along the road just like live people,
and their clothes are not at all old-fashioned.
When I wake up we drive through the early morning mist
past lochs which are as calm as plates.
The sun has not yet risen and the world is quiet.
The roses hang their heads among the dew.

WAITING FOR A LETTER

Every morning she waits for a letter.
Every morning she looks at the mat.
She trembles waiting for a letter.

But there is never any letter.
Every morning the postman passes by
in his world of air and rain.

One morning, she prays, one morning,
let the letter box snap like a dog
at a letter from somewhere
at a letter from anywhere
at a letter wet with rain.

WHEN DAY IS DONE

Sorrow remembers us when day is done.
It sits in its old chair gently rocking
and singing tenderly in the evening.
It welcomes us home again after the day.
It is so old in its black silken dress,
its stick beside it carved with legends.
It tells its stories over and over again.
After a while we have to stop listening.

THE SCREAM

The scream rips through the forest
tearing the trees down.

'Love me love me love me,'
cries the scream at the railway station
with its hair streaming backwards.

It's like a train flashing
at two hundred miles an hour
blowing the birds from the hedges
and bending the iron rails.

It ends up at a cottage
deep in a secret wood
searching the pale windows
for the kind iron face.

It staggers across the flowers
and beats on the warped door
which opens like a cloud
onto its sudden rain.

It crosses the bare floor
like a single moonbeam
and lies in a straight line
on its exhausted paws.

THE NOSE
(after Gogol)

The nose went away by itself
in the early morning
while its owner was asleep.
It walked along the road
sniffing at everything.

It thought: I have a personality of my own.
Why should I be attached to a body?
I haven't been allowed to flower.
So much of me has been wasted.

And it felt wholly free.
It almost began to dance.
The world was so full of scents
it had had no time to notice,

when it was attached to a face
weeping, being blown,
catching all sorts of germs
and changing colour.

But now it was quite at ease
bowling merrily along
like a hoop or a wheel,
a factory packed with scent.

And all would have been well
but that, round about evening,
having no eyes for guides,
it staggered into the path
of a mouth, and it was gobbled
rapidly like a sausage
and chewed by great sour teeth –
and that was how it died.

IN THE MIDDLE

In the middle
flashings,
shakings and glitterings.

Arms that come from the right,
arms that come from the left.

Whispers at corners. 'Is Hamlet better? Is Sarah?
Where are the flowers of spring, ah, where are they?'

Notes that are sent about thunder,
cards about lightning,
chairs that tower like skeletons out of the storm.

Is he well? Is he ill? Bring me my burning chariot,
my helmet, my sceptre, my mail of the yellowest gold.

Arms that come from the right,
papers that come from the left,
posts that breathlessly rush over moorland and road.

What is on fire? Is it my heart? Is it Scotland?
Who is that fellow? Have him put in the stocks
till his hair is singed and his body burns like a crab.

Where is the note I left on top of that tomb?

Someone is painting the walls in a downpour of purple.

Glintings,
shakings,
and flashings.

A postbag of clouds.

THE WHIRLIGIGS OF TIME

The scholar sits by the fire reading.
It's winter and the snow
glares through the window at his book
making it white and himself white,
a fixed and spectral figure.

Two red-cheeked men in leather
enter and take him away.
They unclamp him from his Homer
and from his lamp. The day
is sinister and strange.

'All will be new,' they tell him.
'The political climate's changed.
We are the new seed-sowers.
Blossoms like you must fade
from the flowers that we've arranged.'

And they set him against a wall
dazed in the odd shadows.
He gazes into their colourless eyes
and then falls like a sack
against their quick bullets,

thinking how it's always the same,
the helmet clamped to his brow,
the shield at his pale breast
as he drifts towards Hades
less in rage than sorrow,

and sits there on a chair
with furrowed brow reading
a book on political change
till the two men come in
from the pouring wind and rain

and raising his gaunt head
he pronounces sentence.
'In the great wheel of the seasons
the hawks feed on the swallows
then the swallows on the hawks.'

NONE IS THE SAME AS ANOTHER

None is the same as another,
O none is the same.

That none is the same as another
is matter for crying
since never again will you see
that one, once gone.

In their brown hoods
the pilgrims are crossing the land
and many will look the same
but all are different

and their ideas fly to them
on accidental winds
perching awhile in their minds
from different valleys.

None is the same as another,
O none is the same.

And that none is the same is not
a matter for crying.

Stranger, I take your hand,
O changing stranger.

from MY CANADIAN UNCLE

'I'll take you to see Smith,' he said one day.
'He's never been to church in Canada.
I'll tell you the cause of that. It was this way.
Before he embarked he met the minister.
(It might have been in 1902 or 3.)
The minister told him, I have heard them say
you worked in the Greenock shipyards on a Sunday.
You work on a Sunday yourself, young Smith replied,
and the minister wouldn't speak to him the day
he sailed for Canada. (He was just nineteen.)
What do you think of that? Of course you've been
an atheist from your youth, your mother said.
But God exists, you must remember that.
I'll meet my dearest Mary when I'm dead.
Each year I read the Bible, every word.
There's not a tribe whose name I can't recall.
I'm now at the Letters of the Apostle Paul.
I've got the Bible that my father had
with all our names in it. There is a God.
We go to another country, and we live.'
I listened while he argued with his friend,
who'd never been to church in Canada.
'It was an apple Eve and Adam ate.'
'No,' said Smith, 'it doesn't name the fruit.'
'It was an apple that in Paradise
the snake enticed them to,' my uncle said.

And so they fought
over the apple or the nameless fruit.
'There is a God,' he said. 'You must have faith.
When I was young my mother punished me

for spilling milk on the floor. Did I tell you that?
"You mustn't spill the good fresh milk of God."
So she hung me in a creel above the fire.
By gosh, I felt the burning.'
                                        And Smith said,
'Darwin proved that we all come from apes.'
'Garbage,' my uncle said. 'Have you ever seen
a graceless monkey change into a man.'
'But it's millions of years,' said Smith. 'Millions and more.'
'Garbage,' my uncle said. And Smith went on.
'What use is your appendix. Tell me that.
Darwin has proved that all of us have tails.'
'Tales,' said my uncle mockingly. 'I'd say
you're a bit of an ape yourself, but not me.'
'You're not a scientist,' Smith replied,
limping about the kitchen. For his pride
was punctured by my uncle's mocking laugh.
'These facts are proved.' But my uncle saw him off.
'You'll be saying next it was oranges or grapes
they had in Eden, that they were munched by apes.'
In great good humour he drove home that day.
'Of course he reads a lot but what he says
is garbage pure and simple.'

                                        For his God
was large and merciless, violent, unflawed;
had guided him to Vancouver, from the doss-
houses of Winnipeg, and his gain and loss
were sure and evident. By each lonely grave
as far as the Arctic, God maintained his grave
and ceaseless watch, a munching ghost,
pensive and moony, and no soul was lost
but was herded from the dosshouses to fanks.
From crumby lodgings, oily, grease-embossed,

the unshaven tramps, itinerants, offered thanks,
bowed to the ground. 'O, I love you God
because you scourge me with your vicious rod.'

We sat in the garden among harmless snakes
in Canada, so sunny, without God,
and drank our coffee and ate scones and cake.

This poem was published posthumously but written much earlier.

MY BROTHER

My brother, today the rain is falling,
I haven't heard from you for twenty years.
When you left first you were so confident,
riding your new horse from coast to coast.
Then after a while you stopped writing.
My letters never reached you for you changed addresses.
Were you ashamed that your new horse never lasted?
Sailors from the old country have seen you in bars
but you don't speak to them.
Success is demanded of the exile.
Today as the rain falls it occurred to me
that I do not know where you are.
How the world comes between even two brothers!
All I can see is the horse you wrote of
standing in a cage of rain somewhere
with the burrs of twenty years on its skin.

from *The Emigrants* (1983)

[poems translated from the author's own Gaelic]

WE WILL WALK

We will walk between two verses
where the words will not catch us.

We will walk between two waves
where the sea will not reach us.

We will talk between two languages
where the guilt will not ravage us.

We will walk between two graves
where we will avoid death.

BERRIES

We gathered berries on an autumn day
from trees that grew beside the road.
The ripe ones were behind thorns.
Why is that, you said.
The day was so calm and beautiful,
the berries were like black bells
from which no sound rose.
I looked for my hands, they were entirely red,
as if there was blood on them, bright red blood.
The evening was so calm that I could hear your thoughts
as you walked so carefully among the thorns
with your red boots, with your legs so tall and white.

WHEN I AM READING

When I am reading
the literature of my people
I think,
We have no Homer

no poet as great as that,
at all as great as that,
in that way
in that marvellous way.

But now and again I read
about a particular girl
who died of love
in a ragged dress

or an eagle will rise
crying, I was eating
noble dead soldiers
who were lying on a battlefield.

And now and again there will sail
on the sea towards Canada
ships with salt sails,
songs that are white with pain.

RETURNING EXILE

You who come home do not tell me
anything about yourself, where you have come from,
why your coat is wet, why there is grass in your hair.

The sheep huddle on the hills as always,
there's a yellow light as if cast by helmets,
the fences made of wire are strung by the wind.

Do not tell me where you have come from, beloved stranger.
It is enough that there is light still in your eyes,
that the dog rising on his pillar of black knows you.

THERE IS NO SORROW

There is no sorrow worse than this sorrow
the dumb grief of the exile
among villages that have strange names
among the new rocks.
The shadows are not his home's shadows
nor the tales his tales
and even the sky is not the same
nor the stars at night.

Sometimes he sees his home in the stars
the light from its window
his village trembling and vibrating
and the old white faces
mumbling at the fire.

But the strange names stand up against him
and the dryness of the earth
and the cold barks of dogs
and his sails are folded in this harbour
which is not his.

Poor lost exile
For you there is nothing but endurance
till one miraculous day
you will wake up in the morning
and put on your foreign clothes
and know that they are at last yours.

NEXT TIME

Listen, when you come home
to see your wife again
where the tapestry stands unfinished
across the green brine,
sit among the stones
and consider how it was
in the old days
before you became a king
and walked hunchbacked
with decisions on your shoulders.

Sit among the rocks
hearing the sound of the sea
eternally unchanging
and watch the buttercups
so luminously pale.

The cries of the dead
haunt the gaunt headland
and the shields clash
in that astonishing blue.

Simply enter the boat
and leave the island
for there is no return,
boy, forerunner of kings.

Next time, do this,
salt bronzed veteran
let the tapestry be unfinished
as truthful fiction is.

THE EXILES

(Translated from the author's own Gaelic)

The many ships that left our country
with white wings for Canada.
They are like handkerchiefs in our memories
and the brine like tears
and in their masts sailors singing
like birds on branches.
That sea of May running in such blue,
a moon at night, a sun at daytime,
and the moon like a yellow fruit,
like a plate on a wall
to which they raise their hands
like a silver magnet
with piercing rays
streaming into the heart.

WHEN MY POETRY MAKING HAS FAILED

When my poetry making has failed
I sit in the middle of autumn like a black clock
uselessly ticking.
I try to sing
inside my glazed armour,
a tortoise on fire.
But nothing saves me except for the water that runs
harmlessly and without herald
from some place that I have been and cannot remember
where the words stand around like rocks.

SPEECH FOR A WOMAN

One night
I saw my children
climbing the stairs in the frost

which had carved an unintelligible language
on the single window.

'Where have you been?' I asked
for they were whistling
and talking about the magic games they had played
in green ferocious shirts.

'Everywhere,' they said.
'Especially where the blue sky blackens
under the weight of the seas:
and particularly in a desert from which we saw
a woman in a brown shawl waving.
Ships we took, trains we took, and the green buses
that flowed across a country under siege
where the same women with their empty mouths
spoke of eternal famine.'

The whistling faded.
I opened their room.
It was tidier than I had ever seen it.

The sweaty socks were not to be seen
nor the embroidered jerseys,
nor the records with the satanic drums
nor the pictures.

It was a ruined shrine that I was looking at.
Slowly the clock began to tick

And it flowed through my whole body
which was a dress of sand
emptying like an hourglass as I gazed.

AUSTRALIA

1

In Australia the trees are deathly white,
the kangaroos are leaping halfway to heaven
but land at last easily on the earth.
Sometimes I hear graves singing
their Gaelic songs to the dingos
which scrabble furiously at the clay.
Then tenderly in white they come towards me,
drifting in white, the far exiles
buried in the heart of brown deserts.
It is a strange language they speak
not Australian not Gaelic
while the green eyes stalk them
under a moon the same as ours
but different, different.

2

Naturally there are photographs of Ned Kelly
in his iron mask in his iron armour.
His iron body hung stiffly in the wind
which blew past the ravens.
In that dry land his armour will not rust
and the hot sun flashes from it
as if it were a mirror, creator of fresh stars.
However dingos leap at it they will not chew him
for he is a story, a poem,
a tale that is heard on the wind.

3

No, you will not return from Australia
however you may wish to do so.
For you have surrendered to its legend,
to its music being continually reborn,
to the eerie whine of its deserts.
Somehow or another it entered your soul
and however much you remember Scotland,
its graves sanctified by God,
its historical darknesses,
you will not return from it.
Its dust is in your nostril,
its tenderness has no justice,
its millions of stars are the thoughts
of unbridled horsemen.
With blue eyes you will stare
blinded into its blueness
and when you remember your rivers,
the graveyards the mountains,
it is Australia that stands up in front of you,
your question, your love.

4

All day the kookaburra is laughing
from the phantoms of trees,
from the satire of nature.
It is not tragedy nor comedy,
it is the echo of beasts,
the bitter chorus of thorns,
and flowers that have names
that aren't easily remembered.

The kookaburra laughs from the trees,
from the branches of ghosts,
but the sky remains blue
and the eyes glow green in the night.

NO RETURN

No, really you can't go back to
that island any more. The people
are growing more and more unlike you
and the fairy stories
have gone down to the grave in peace.

The wells are dry now and the long grasses
parched by their mouths, and the horned cows
have gone away to another country
where someone else's imagination
is fed daily on milk.

There were, you remember, sunsets
against which the black crows were seen
and a moonlight of astonishing beauty
calmed at midnight by waters
which you're not able to hear.

The old story-telling people
have gone home to their last houses
under the acres of a lost music.
These have all been sold now
to suave strangers with soft voices.

It is a great pity, that your cottage
preserved in January by clear ice
and in June surrounded by daisies
has been sold to the same strangers
and the bent witches evicted.

If you were to return now the roofs
would appear lower, the walls would have no echoes,
the wavelike motion would be lost,
the attics where you read all day
would be crammed with antiques.

No, you cannot return to an island
expecting that the dances will be unchanged,
that the currency won't have altered,
that the mountains blue in the evening
will always remain so.

You can't dip your mouth in the pure spring
ever again or ever again be haunted
by the 'eternal sound of the ocean'.
Even the boats which you once rowed
have set off elsewhere.

The witches wizards harlequins jesters
have packed up their furniture and guitars.
The witches have gone home on their broomsticks
and the conjurors with their small horses
and tiny carts have departed

leaving the island bare, bleak and windy,
itself alone in its barren corner
composed of real rocks and real flowers
indifferent to the rumours and the stories
stony, persistent.

READING SHAKESPEARE

On a dark day in winter I read Shakespeare.
The birds set off to branches of the south.
I tremble in the branches of the mind.

Summer is finished. Shakespeare always remains,
tree on tree for ever fragrant, young,
leaves that never fall out of the leaves.

Forest of Arden, you are my best south,
the lightning wit in this locality,
the cloudless sky, the rainbow tunics there,

and thunder too. We have the best of it,
so many weathers, changeable, intense.
Farewell to the long-necked geese that cross the sea.

SPEECH FOR PROSPERO

When I left that island I thought I was dead. Nothing
stirred in me. Miranda in jeans
and totally innocent was standing by a sail
and all the others happily recovered talking
in suits made of brine. But to return to
the gossip, the poisonous ring, was not easy,
and many times I nearly tried to turn back
feeling in my bones the desolate hum of the headland,
my creation of rivers and mist.
Still we went on. The corruption had put on flesh,
the young were hopeful again, all was forgiven.
Nevertheless the waiters were scraping and bowing,
the rumours beginning, the crowns of pure crystal were sparkling,
the telephones were ringing with messages from the grave
and the thin phosphorescent boys glowing with ambition
in corners of velvet and death.
Still I went on. The ship left its wake behind it,
shining and fading, cord of a new birth,
and over by the rail Miranda gazed at her prince
yearning for love.
Goodbye, island, never again shall I see you,
you are part of my past. Though I may dream of you often
I know there's a future we all must learn to accept,
music working itself out in the absurd halls and the mirrors,
posturings of men like birds, Art in a torrent of plates,
the sound of the North Wind, distant yet close,
as stairs ascend from the sea.

'YOU'LL TAKE A BATH'

'And now you'll take a bath,' she'd always say,
just when I was leaving, to keep me back.
At the second turning of the stony stair
the graffiti were black letters in a book
misspelt and menacing. As I drove away
she'd wave from the window. How could I always bear
to be her knight abandoning her to her tower
each second Sunday, a ghost that was locked fast
in a Council scheme, where radios played all day
unknown raw music, and young couples brought
friends home to midnight parties, and each flower
in the grudging garden died in trampled clay.

Standing by her headstone in the mild
city of bell-less doors, I feel the sweat
stink my fresh shirt out, as each gravelly path
becomes a road, long lost, in a bad bet.
Once more I see the dirty sleepy child.
'The water's hot enough. You'll have a bath.'

And almost I am clean but for that door
so blank and strong, imprinted with her name
as that far other in the scheme was once,
and 'scheme' becomes a mockery, and a shame,
in this neat place, where each vase has its flower,
and the arching willow its maternal stance.

BRUEGEL

A bony horse with a bird on it droops its head.
With a cart of skulls like potatoes Death drives onward.

There's a storm of monsters snouted and obscene
and on another page a neat snow scene.

Large peasants dance under a leaden sky
and ships are sinking in a black-framed sea.

The blind raise tortured faces. In Cockayne
they eat and drink and sleep and at the moon

a peasant pisses. Proverbs multiply.
Children with adult faces gravely play

while aprons break the storm, red plates and jugs,
Death in a hood and lands pulled back like rugs.

And over the countryside the black birds go
with far below them hunters in the snow.

This poem also appears in an earlier collection, *Orpheus and Other Poems.*

OWL AND MOUSE

The owl wafts home with a mouse in its beak.
The moon is stunningly bright in the high sky.

Such a gold stone, such a brilliant hard light.
Such large round eyes of the owl among the trees.

All seems immortal but for the dangling mouse,
an old hurt string among the harmony

of the masterful and jewelled orchestra
which shows no waste soundlessly playing on.

'IOLAIRE'

[On New Year's Eve 1918 a ship called the Iolaire *left Kyle of Lochalsh to bring three hundred men home to Lewis after the war was over. On New Year's morning 1919 the ship went on the rocks as a result of a navigational error at the Beasts of Holm, a short distance from Stornoway, the main town on the island. About two hundred sailors were drowned. In the following poem I imagine an elder of the church speaking as he is confronted with this mind-breaking event.]*

The green washed over them. I saw them when
the New Year brought them home. It was a day
that orbed the horizon with an enigma.
It seemed that there were masts. It seemed that men
buzzed in the water round them. It seemed that fire
shone in the water which was thin and white
unravelling towards the shore. It seemed that I
touched my fixed hat which seemed to float and then
the sun illumined fish with naval caps,
names of the vanished ships. In sloppy waves,
in the fat of water, they came floating home
bruising against their island. It is true,
a minor error can inflict this death.
That star is not responsible. It shone
over the puffy blouse, the flapping blue
trousers, the black boots. The seagull swam
bonded to the water. Why not man?
The lights were lit last night, the tables creaked
with hoarded food. They willed the ship to port
in the New Year which would erase the old,
its errant voices, its unpractised tones.
Have we done ill, I ask, my fixed body
a simulacrum of the transient waste,
for everything was mobile, planks that swayed,

the keeling ship exploding and the splayed
cold insect bodies. I have seen your church
solid. This is not. The water pours
into the parting timbers where I ache
above the globular eyes. The slack heads turn
ringing the horizon without sound,
with mortal bells, a strange exuberant flower
unknown to our dry churchyards. I look up.
The sky begins to brighten as before,
remorseless amber, and the bruised blue grows
at the erupting edges. I have known you, God,
not as the playful one but as the black
thunderer from hills. I kneel
and touch this dumb blonde head. My hand is scorched.
Its human quality confuses me.
I have not felt such hair so dear before
nor seen such real eyes. I kneel from you.
This water soaks me. I am running with
its tart sharp joy. I am floating here
in my black uniform. I am embraced
by these green ignorant waters. I am calm.

FOR POETS WRITING IN ENGLISH OVER IN IRELAND

'Feeling,' they said,
'that's the important thing' –
those poets who write in English over in Ireland.

It was late.
There was dancing in the hall,
playing of pipes, of bones, of the penny whistle.

They were an island in that Irishness.
'Larkin and Dunn,' they said. 'Now Dunn is open
to more of the world than ageing Larkin is.

What room was Mr Bleaney in? It's like
going to any tenement and finding
any name you can think of on the door.

And you wonder a little about him but not much.'
We were sitting on the floor outside the room
where a song in Irish waltzed the Irish round.

Do the stones, the sea, seem different in Irish?
Do we walk in language, in a garment pure
as water? Or as earth just as impure?

The grave of Yeats in Sligo, Innisfree
island seen shivering on an April day.
The nuns who cycle down an Easter road.

The days are beads strung on a thin wire.
Language at Connemara is stone
and the water green as hills is running westwards.

The little children in the primary school
giggling a little at our Scottish Gaelic,
writing in chalk the Irish word for 'knife'.

To enter a different room. When did Bleaney
dance to the bones? This world is another world.
A world of a different language is a world

we find our way about in with a stick,
half-deaf half-blind, snatching a half word there,
seeing a twisted figure in a mirror,

slightly unnerved, unsure. I must go home.
To English? Gaelic? O beautiful Maud Gonne,
the belling hounds spoke in what language to you?

In that tall tower so finished and so clear
his international name was on the door
and who would ask who had been there before him?

I turn a page and read an Irish poem
translated into English and it says
(the poet writing of his wife who'd died):

'Half of my eyes you were, half of my hearing,
half of my walking you were, half of my side.'
From what strange well are these strange words upspringing?

But then I see you, Yeats, inflexible will,
creator of yourself, a conscious lord,
writing in English of your own Maud Gonne.

Inside the room there's singing and there's dancing.
Another world is echoing with its own
music that's distant from the world of Larkin.

And I gaze at the three poets. They are me,
poised between two languages. They have chosen
with youth's superb confidence and decision.

'Half of my side you were, half of my seeing,
half of my walking you were, half of my hearing.'
Half of this world I am, half of this dancing.

POEM

It is always evening in a German poem,
the moon shining on the shell-like houses
and the roses like swans' necks bowed over lakes.

Something is always about to happen,
a crouched being rising over the horizon
with fur on its hands and fur about its cheeks.

Past the water it comes, out of the moonlight,
heading steadily past the little church,
the tavern that resounds with loud tunes.

And it stands, turning its head in the moonlight,
slowly, purposefully, in the pure light
among the roses with the necks of swans

while somewhere in the distance a bell rings
very gently, humbly, and a milkmaid
sings to herself, the warm pail in her hand.

THE SURVIVORS

How can they survive the days
those who have no talent
how can they face the sharpness of the morning star?

Those who have no direction
who have nothing they can do well
whose days do not form a book

or even a particular style
such that it feeds on the clouds
and on the big spaces between them.

Admire them most of all
those who built the pyramids
but were too close to them to see.

Those who died
before the road was completed
before the bridge spanned the water.

The hyphens the dashes the strokes –
those who see the sunsets
as wheels that return and return.

These I think are the true heroes,
they push stones away from their breasts
when they rise in the morning.

THE ‘ORDINARY’ PEOPLE

The ‘ordinary’ people sing on the edge of the grave.
When the hero howls and cries they are humming
in the middle of ropes, griefs, the deaths of roses.

The ‘ordinary’ people are not stones.
They are revengeful, bitter, quick to strike and laugh
and they buy oranges at the market-place.

The ‘ordinary’ people say, ‘I’ll not be put upon.’
They spend their money freely on food and drink
and then they have no money, only hope.

Where does the hope come from that they see,
who live precariously by the deaths of roses,
and hang their washing among tragedies?

I begin to think there are no ‘ordinary’ people.

Or rather that they’ve learned about tragedies
from birth and can simply pass them by
or walk through them clutching food, bottles.

I believe there is no such thing as tragedy,
that the hero has deceived us, is the red infant
howling and screaming from his wooden cage.

AT THE FUNERAL OF ROBERT GARIOCH

Something about the April day
touched me
as they slid your coffin onto the trolley
in the Crematorium.

More and more often it troubles me
this wind my sails have missed
which is still around me
fluttering the bluebells.

'The Lord's My Shepherd' we sang.
It was time for the burning.
The minister blessed it
dressed in his white gown,

his voice fat and voluptuous,
his enunciation pure.
You slid down into fire
in your yellow coffin.

In half-way April
the breeze was vulnerable
straying among the warble
of the first birds.

Poet, the flowers are open
even when we are dead
even when the power has gone
from our right arms.

The flowers open in flame.
The coffin slides home.
Fugitive April becomes
a tremendous summer.

WHO DAILY

Who daily at the rickety table
writes and sings, writes and sings,
Venus with the one arm,
Apollo with the one leg,
the stuttering rainbow that hirples
like early crayons into the sea.

ENVOI

There are
more things in heaven and earth, Horatio,
than bones, roses. There are windows
through which gaunt faces peer
and there are children
running through great doors.
Consider
how the sea roars mournfully at the edge of
all things, how the seaweed
hangs at the sailor's neck, the crab
shuffles in armour, Horatio,
thc punctual dead visit us, rise
bird-voiced from the grass,
and the owls
are scholars of the woods.
Horatio, I remember
a kingdom and a kingdom's diplomat,
a girl floating tenderly down stream,
a crown on her young head.
These are portents, warnings, ominous
reflections from the mirror.
Horatio
my eyes darken. Tragedy is
nothing but churned foam.
I wave to you
from this secure and leafy entrance,
this wooden
door on which I bump my head,
this moment and then,
that.

from A LIFE

Lewis 1928–45 (4)

You will not find a Rubens, Rembrandt here,
nor my revered Vermeer. You will not find
the velvet-lined
hound faces of aristocrats: the blind
blank mask of genius with its gravid stare.

The meagre furniture appals me here,
the props of rock, of heather, and of sea,
the constancy
of ruined walls and nettles. A humming bee
is smartly burning round an absent pier.

Life without art, the minimum. I hear
a sermon tolling, for your theatre is
the fire of grace,
hypothesis of hell, a judging face
looming from storm towards boats and sea-drenched gear,

the thrifty fields, monotonous, austere,
where poppies are superfluous, and the rose.
The thistle grows
its thorny purple crown: and Sunday flows
with its burning transient girls through psalm and prayer.

Aberdeen University 1945–49 (1)

The glitter of the water and the wake…
Heading for University in Aberdeen.
It's an autumn morning. I am seventeen.
Above the Isle of Skye the dawn's a flag

of red infuriate ore. I see the train
for the first time ever steaming from the Kyle
beyond the screaming seagulls, in the smell
of salt and herring. There's a tall sad crane.

The landscape, rich, harmonious, unwinds
its perfect symmetry: not the barren stone
and vague frail fences I have always known.
I hold my Homer steady in my hand.

All day we travel and at last dismount
at the busy station of that sparkling town.
A beggar with black glasses sitting down
on the hard stone holds out his cap. I count

the pennies in it. Should I freely give?
Or being more shameful than himself refrain?
His definite shadow is the day's black stain.
How in such open weakness learn to live?

I turn away, the money in my hand,
profusely sweating, in that granite blaze.
Unknown, unlooked at, I pick up my case.
Everything's glittering and transient.

National Service 1950–52 (1)

The corporal struts briskly up and down,
moustached, Hitlerian. 'You play fair with me
and I'll play fair with you. Otherwise...'
We stand at attention in the barrack room
beside our beds. There's a black ancient stove.
The sentry at the gate had glassy boots
and glassy eyes. The reapers in the fields
waved towards us as we trudged the dusty road
in the last hot July of our free youth.
We lay in our grave sheets as the Last Post
wailed through the room, a lost mysterious soul,
the bugle music of our homesickness.
The lights of our windows faded towards the square
where the RSM, a brutal cockerel,
had shouted as we trudged towards the door
which shut on Milton and on Shakespeare.

Clydebank and Dumbarton 1952–55 (3)

The flash of trains on rails, the Cenotaph,
how shall these meet, collide?

Pale girls at evening on neon roads –
the marble halls of Rome.

Cloth-capped Glaswegians with their spotted hounds –
great Homer in his pride.

The vested hairy-chested boilerman
soaping his body in the kitchen sink –
the libraries and tomes.

And yet as legionaries they once set out
thump thump on knife-straight roads,

creating once their strong geometries
to link damp hut and hut.

Oban 1955-82 (2)

A Roman rector, measured gravitas,
a Gaelic scholar too. He knows each child.
Our own names honour us and each one salutes

us from his sparkling bicycle. The school hums,
directed engine. Black-winged he comes
along the shiny corridors. In the hall

appointing prefects he quotes from Paul.
The race is to the kind, not to the smart,
to Brutus not to Antony. The clear art

of human Homer is our constant aim:
whatever's comely. Casually he says,
'It was Housman taught me in my Cambridge days.'

And behind him MacIntyre and William Ross.
Where's Eliot and Auden? Horace glows,
each marble phrase, the clarity of prose.

'Transposing Greek to Gaelic is no toil.
They had their clans, their sea terms. And the style
of the great *Odyssey* is what Gaelic knows.'

Easily he chats to the crofting man
who sucks a straw: as easily as he scans
those vast hexameters or the pibroch.

Does
what's comely and what's right by natural rule,
by Roman cheerfulness and harmonious Greek.
Propounds a human yet a rigorous school.

Taynuilt 1982– (16)

There is no island.
The sea unites us.
The salt is in our mouth.

I have heard the drowned sing
when the moonlight
casts a road across the waters,
fine and luminous,
and each house sways
in its autumn light.

'The moon that takes us home to Lewis.'
to the dancing
to the phantoms of evening
to the charmed wells.

The island, as our poet said,
is an iceberg.
We bear it with us,
our flawed jewel.

As the sun sets
over the mountains
I see the homeless ones
forever rowing.
Their peasant hats mushroom,
like foundering bouquets.

The wakes
are for everyone
and the large sun
glints on the excised names
of the exiles.

‘No ebb tide ever came
without a full tide after it’ –
precious ones
whose flesh is my own,

and who arise each day
to a new desert.

The island, my vase, knows you.
Your inscribed faces
burn out of the brine:
this is the sharp wine
that educates us.

As we change
so the island changes,
we are not estranged
by the salt billows.

‘There is no ebb tide
without a full tide after it.’
The tall white bride
accepts the fresh waters.

from THE VILLAGE

21

Death strides freely across the countryside,
    swinging his stick.
Sometimes he stops at a cottage
    where an old woman
is fraying fresh water
    from a bucket.
Sometimes he watches a weasel
    sucking the throat of a hare
    beside a rowan tree.
Sometimes he watches a cat
    trotting with a lark
    through the shrubbery.
He takes out a cigarette and smokes it,
    a small cloud at his mouth
    and listens to a radio
    playing Greensleeves.
Sometimes he knocks on a door
    of a large house
    where a man with white hair
    is reading Everyman.
Death is a polite fellow
    who loves azaleas
    and the blur of bluebells.
'Without me they would not exist
    without my sickle and scythe
    without my empty circles.
And what would the shepherd be then
    singing of his sweetheart?
    And as for Greece or Rome,
    beyond the Dark Ages
they shine like jewels of fire.'

VILLAGERS

So many of those that I once knew
drowned in the Atlantic or the Pacific,
that unignorable and unknown blue.

Fishermen and part-time footballers,
inadequate scholars, starers at dusty maps,
now forever locked in the sea's purse

with a miserly snap, while the guns tolled
over these restless acres, not to be ploughed,
at sunset fading into a foreign gold.

These guns which defended an empire
which wasn't, isn't, yours, who have drowned
ignorantly in sharp salt and fire,

who were once big figures in the twilight
where the river gently ran and chimneys bloomed
with a smoke sometimes grey and sometimes violet,

bone of my bone, my villagers. You have met
with the foreign-spoken stranger who has pulled
you inwards to his boat, his teeming net,

a random catch, I think not predestined,
gaping, slack-jawed, stubbly. Yet I sing
you breathless in the meshes long enchained.

PHOTOGRAPH OF EMIGRANTS

Your faces cheerful though impoverished,
you stand at the rail, tall-collared and flat-capped.
You are leaving Lewis (Stornoway) behind.
Before you the appalling woods will rise
after the sea's sharp salt, your axes hack
the towering trunks. What are you leaving now? –
The calm routine of winding chimney smoke,
the settled village with its small sparse fields,
the ceilidhs and the narratives. Deceived
by chiefs and lairds, by golden promises,
you set off, smiling towards a new world,
Canada with its Douglas firs and snow,
its miles of desolate emptiness.

Why do I weep
to see these faces, thin and obsolete,
these Sunday ties and collars, by the rail,
as the ship moves, and you move with it,
towards your flagrant destinies of sharp
bony starvation, ruinous alcohol.

All shall be revealed but at this time
your faces blaze with earnestness, and joy,
as if you were coming home instead of leaving.
Nothing will save some, standing by the rail,
others will come home in tartan caps,
a fury of possessions, and a love
of what's disappeared forever when they left,
themselves not being able to be there and here,
and therefore growing differently towards pictures
which frame them where they stand, thus staring out
into the inscrutable waters of their fates.

INCUBATOR

The tiny baby sleeps in a cage of wires.
Lights blink on and off:

its legs are thin as matches, and its hair
a fuzz of limpid gold.

Sometimes it arches its tiny body,
stretches itself and yawns,

delicate as an egg in that machinery
which sings its own quiet tune.

Machine, you are my mother now, you feed
with the slow drop of time.

It is warm here, sleepless mother,
raise me to run one day

with my leather schoolbag among blossoms
on a day of lessons and fire.

Wakeful machinery, be good to me,
hear me if I don't breathe,

and ring your alarm bell, the panic
of your kind breast of steel.

Machine, let us sleep together,
on the bosom of the night,

till I grow tall, till I leave you
and seek soft human arms.

THE STORY

This is the story that I've always loved.
A little girl is running towards a bridge.
She leaves her tiny footprints in the snow,
and then suddenly becomes invisible.

Like the reader who leaves off reading the page,
Like the dying who have still some way to go.
There are first the footprints, then the unfathomable.
The Muse hasn't finished the good poem.

Perhaps it isn't good enough; perhaps
another poem takes over, yet another
better and more invisible song will come
out of the snow with a flaring of red banners.

Perhaps one day the ending will come back.
Now we aren't finished, but some day
after fresh experience we will find it,
having first tumbled from the bridge,

which is a rainbow from white heaven to here.
The little girl is ageing somewhere else.
She has run through a mirror to a new country.
Drenched and flecked with snow, she has changed.

What is the future? Suddenly it breaks off.
This is a part of freedom, isn't it?
Years later she appears, no more a child,
but adult, unperplexed, her own mother.

Rainbow I love you, you are composed of light,
primary colours, hiatuses, a bridge.
Athlete and artist, you have perfectly curved
into the rich ignorance of the future.

AT THE PARTY

At the party everyone is talking.
Suddenly silence falls and you are alone
among the plates, the wine-glasses, the cups.
And there is no one to talk to but a limping man
who comes in late smoking a cigarette.
His face is gaunt and his frosty hair is wet.
And he coughs repeatedly and he says,
'This is my fifth party tonight.
I am rather tired and my appetite
is not as good as it used to be.'

And there he is, graduate of frost and snow,
coughing repeatedly and saying No.

AFTER THE EDINBURGH FESTIVAL

The Festival is over,
the Chinese acrobats have gone home
tumbling over piles of chairs across Europe,
dangling from the autumn skies.

Hamlet, wrapped in his black cloak, is brooding
among the colourful courts of the clouds,
hearing behind the curtains of leaves
a mortal song.

The Finnish poet has stopped reading
and is back among the pines
which stand like masts beside the lakes
in the country of the strange tongue.

The paintings hang in a gallery of the wind
showing harbours, people,
squares of an autumnal colour,
on which the night is falling.

The black troupe has returned to South Africa
and the sour smell of prisons,
their passes held humbly in their hands
in the debris of desolate camps.

Autumn remembers art
and the pipers who played at the castle
in a swish of sculpture
among the historical deaths.

Listen, is that the dry cold music of Stravinsky
bony, intellectual,
and the king in his suit of plague
bleeding volubly from the eyes.

Clowns, acrobats, actors,
you are our marvellous doubles
you keep the autumnal ice away
from the pools of evening.

You sing so high that the ice will break,
you put the dazzling crown from you,
your power is different,
yours is the glitter of cloaks,

the tinsel that illuminates the meagre,
the masks that face both ways,
the Januaries of ambiguity,
the consolation of defects.

And the acrobats on the edge of disaster
are saved by strong wrists,
and the lady who was sawn in half
jumps to her feet.

Resurrections, deaths, resurrections,
who is that black blind visitor
who sits patiently by the fire,
mortal ventriloquist,

whose tenement is falling apart,
while the stuttering landlord
is hopelessly free of his speech
in a room that is bordered with leaves?

MEETING

I'm sure you don't know me, she said,
putting out her arms to me. On a wet day
in Lewis this was, among the dead.

Surely I know you, and she smiled.
You're Jessie, I said, and you stayed
in my village when I was a child.

So glad she was I remembered her, though dead,
her hair combed with salt, her hands
remembering the clothes pegs she would fit

to the line once with her gallery of frocks.
Woolworths where we stood shone red.
I grew tired, she said, of the white clocks,

but you, you're different. And her mouth spread
like a seagull's in the wet and briny day.
I emigrated to the sea from dry land,

the waves attracted me with their energy.
But this is spring, isn't it, she said,
if you remember that clear cloudless sky

with no clothes in it. Yes, don't shed
tears, I answered. There is memory.
And took her fading hands. We are wed

to springs, autumns, visible and solid.
And watched her fade and fade past Woolworths' red
imitation jewels, like a seaward bird.

GIRL AND CHILD

Trudging through the air of Homer for a sight of the bruised girl with the child
who stops at kiosks to wait for a telephone to ring
with his voice out of the clouds that have grown suddenly callous,
and a ring which she has not yet sold winking on her finger,
and the child's blue eyes staring out of its temporary nest,
I found only the scene where Andromache holds her child up to Hector
and with small fingers it touches the big shadowy helmet
before his death in a whirl of vulnerable dust.
And the battle is different and for the girl there is no Homer
and there is no memorial among the slums and lights of the city
as she stares into the windows at the bridal dresses and the furs
and slowly licks her lips as if she was tasting the last of her milk.

POOR ARTIST

You who live on the dole and haunt the Oxfam shops,
how do you survive?

In the galleries there are paintings by Vermeer,
there are portraits of the opulent.

But how shall angel feathers spring from worn shoes,
and how shall the Madonna smile at you?

You have no room for a studio,
you must starve for your fresh paints.

And the landscapes look back at you without mercy,
and the still-lives have no serenity.

Let you paint the wine bottles of others,
the sweet apples on their plates,

Let you paint space without boundaries,
the sombre faces of the great.

How should art rise from the pavements,
sparse, moneyless, dizzy.

How should you not be troubled by the smile of the Mona Lisa
by her expensive raiment?

The mystery is in the stones,
the mystery is in the ungovernable,

the desire for permanence.

So that clutching your paints you descend
to the Hades of the chaotic,

and in your mind a table without knives on it,
a table of perfect colour,

and on your feet the worn shoes you must paint,
the remedy of the actual.

AGAINST APARTHEID (II)

For you who have died in the silence of prisons, what prayers are enough?
For you who have been beaten to death,

who will never see the blossoms of your pain, the fruit of your broken bones,
the open and scented windows...

You are the alarm clocks that have been hammered by tyranny,
you are the complex wristwatches that rough hands cannot bear,
you are the imaginative ones.

I see you in the concentrated lights, blinking, exhausted,
I see you staring into the ardours of the future.

You have been accused of arching your bodies through windows like rainbows,
you have been accused of loving death.

Who loved life too much, its perfumes, its radiances,
who hated the cruelty of boots.

Who stared into eyes that have communed with stones
and for whom the human body is plasticine,

a pliable instrument from which all the music has been squeezed,
a careless melodeon.

You who have died in darkness may the future brighten,
for you who have died in silence may there be applause.

I say that your coffins will blossom with roses
when the earth will have devoured your enemies,

and that your bloodstained scripts will outlive their graffiti,
and that your triumph will be heard in the cells of violence,

and that your meagre calendar will be the beginnings of seasons
which will glow brilliantly in your broken spectacles.

SNOW

Snow brings the soul to our land.
It brings the whiteness of eternity, it brings
a book with no print.

Snow, you are so lovely, you frame houses,
you lie in little white hills on the roofs,
you are the genial dictator of the night.

Slowly, gently, you transform the world
as from evil into good,
as from graffiti into origins.

The slums have disappeared, the rivers are silent,
the farms on the moors have become magical houses,
at which we call with white maps on our coats.

Only the spires out-soar the snow,
only the planes which travel sparkling,
only the sun which glows like a forge.

See, she plunges her hands into snow
who belongs to Africa,
whose poverty has not been hidden by it;
she drinks of its coolness.

And the children too enter this new country.
They build snowmen,
they put pipes in their mouths,
red buttons for noses.

Who does not love you, snow?
Magician of the night,
radical reformer,
instant utopianist.
Let us imagine you are eternal,
marvellous painter and sculptor,
let us sing your praises,
forgetting you are common water.

EARLY SPRING

The primroses are out already
at the beginning of January.

And I have heard the birds sing.

Like Chaucer,
like the beginning of an idea,
like the hinge of a horizon.

Like happiness.
Like hearing the click of your heels
on the road outside my house.

And then as you climbed the stairs
your dress of yellow.

FAREWELL MY BROTHER

'Farewell my brother.'
The seas separate us,
a history of salt.

It is as if I had dreamed
that on an island ringed by waves
we once walked

when the buttercups blew in the wind
around the ruins of houses
in a blank sea-gaze.

The Bible was a hard wall
which we climbed over
to touch the consolations of the heart.

Eternal voyaging!
Among the civil wars of Africa
you spent the best of your days.

You will lie in a different earth
far from Lewis
unlearned in your history,
with its own legends.

In the early morning
I heard a raven
squawking above my ground,
a rancorous wanderer
in his bad-tempered province.

Forgive us our misunderstandings.
'Life is not like strolling,
carelessly through a field.'

It is not sunset
over a stubble
colouring the sharpness,
a perfection of swords.

The earth shakes
often when we are surest
of the prosperity of our fortune.

Even when the moon
is round as a coin,
our achieved gamble.

Even as I wrote
you were absently sleeping
like an alien on this earth.

My distant brother
with your own casket
of joys and tribulations.

Barer than the mind
is the soil of Lewis.
It is in the keeping of the wind.
It has the sea's resonance,

that constant music
that enchanted cottage
which enhanced our residence,

our hunger for the unknown.
If we could speak again
would we know better?

I offer this bouquet
from the oceans of salt,
my distant brother.

I send it across the seas
to the spaciousness of Canada,
my flowering poem,

to let its fragrance
be sweet in your nostrils,
though you are now unable
to converse with me.

My distant brother,
in the shelter of my poem
let you be secret

till we are children again
in the one bed
in the changing weather
of an inquisitive childhood.

The roads separate:
see, I wave to you,
you turn away completely
into your own cloud.

See, I wave to you
you are disappearing forever.
Tears disarm me.

Now you stand like a statue
in the honour of goodness.

My pride and my tears burn me.

Farewell, my brother.

LISTEN

Listen, I have flown through darkness towards joy,
I have put the mossy stones away from me,
and the thorns, the thistles, the brambles.
I have swum upward like a fish

through the black wet earth, the ancient roots
which insanely fight with each other
in a grave which creates a treasure house
of light upward-springing leaves.

Such joy, such joy! Such airy drama
the clouds compose in the heavens,
such interchange of comedies,
disguises, rhymes, dénouements.

I had not believed that the stony heads
would change to actors and actresses,
and that the grooved armour of statues
would rise and walk away

into a resurrection of villages,
townspeople, citizens, dead exiles,
who sing with the salt in their mouths,
winged nightingales of brine.

POETRY

Poetry has nothing to do with who we are.
It cannot be explained by biography,
e.g. sickness, unhappiness.
Poetry is a swart planet
with which we are in touch, from which
we receive at certain times messages.
Nor is it a black or emerald clock –
I think it is a voice which speaks to us
at night as unquiet trembling, or maybe
a curious arrangement of stones,
poorly random and yet sonorous,
a packet of crisps beside a Greek vase
on a day with a breeze flowing from the south.

DOGMAS

Perfidious dogmas,
unremitting theses,
let the wild seas
blow through you

with their salt taste
and tang of seaweed
and all the dead
whose bones have been picked clean

by the fresh currents,
and let the rocks of dogma
be steadily worn down
till only the water

brilliantly sparkling
with its modern ships
flows always eastward
towards a temporary sun.

COME, FOOL

Come, fool, and tell me of your successes
just here where the wind combs the grasses
by this cemetery with its wooden crosses.

Come, gold-buttoned fool, with your new car
shining like a crab: walk over
this ancestral ground with its white flowers,

and talk in your loud voice of your gains,
your Midas jacket. Do you not feel the presence
of the empty-mouthed dead, and the dance

of the extinct girls.
                                        Come, glassy fool,
stand by this stone and see your own name

excised as in your schooldays, an address
from your poor cottage to the universe

and then to your Mercedes and your hearse.

THE WILL

I must change my will.
I am not happy with the one
that I have written.

I should have left my money
to those whom I have wronged,
even the dead

who are standing at my bedside
with gaunt faces
and unforgiving eyes.

My breath
is like a train racing
towards an unimaginable station

where the stationmaster,
I think in sea blue,
has gold buttons.

But I am trembling
with the weight of my sins
though God is more than a lawyer

in a blue or grey day.
I am frightened.
Give me the pen.

Let me consider
a bequest to my father
whom I often disobeyed

and to that young girl
I once abandoned
in a ditch of sharp scent

and to my wife
who sits in a black chair
endlessly smiling

like a distraught doll.
The dead are really those
whom I wish to reward

for their vast patience
and for the wounds
I see in their eyes.

And above all
let what money I have
be for my comrades

who in far countries
or in red Flanders
died when young,

my imperfect comrades,
laughing and singing,
who opened beer bottles

in their new suits
working clothes, uniforms,
in fields of fresh grass.

THE OLD POET

Before I go over the horizon of the dark
let me do my last poetry reading in a hall
where there are no excuses from the chairman,
and the room is full of fragrance. And people cry
to think of their bones shining towards evening.
And the hall is crammed with leafy presences,
the dead, the living, and all who were friends to me
when I grew up in the hot mists of June.
And like Eurydice I'll say farewell to them
as I'm gathered to the shades in the lyre's sound
and the steps climb steadily towards a daylight
which I shall never see as my wings fold.

SOMETIMES I REMEMBER

Sometimes I remember the poor relations
in these huge Russian novels, at the edge of
the loud action, with their threadbare gloves
endlessly sitting in rooms while the spurred counts
stride quickly in and out. Poor relations,
no one listens to you, your voices are so faint,
no one can hear you, and you sit there
in the hollow quietness like aspidistras
in their Victorian bowls. Elsewhere,
there is the noise of gunnery, oaths,
men parting tearfully with silver watches,
medallions, in the wind. The horses gulping
for air, pure air. The big book expanding
from fields where a whole class died. No,
no one listens to you. They rush out shouting
pointing at the smoke, and as you wait
white carved ceilings fall and pictures melt,
countesses are rushing through the fire
parasols over their heads.

THE WELL

The children are haunted by the well.
They brim the bucket with pure water,
and pour it over the tilted rim
in a wasteful avalanche of laughter.

There is a well in my mind's eye
we visited with our two pails,
in summer's brilliant brief glory.
Its eye was large and round and chill.

The children jump with happy glee.
This is our story: gravity pulls
us closer to the grassy ground.
But in our youth delighted bubbles

rise in us without a reason.
We are so wasteful of our days.
The serene eye will keep its season
reflecting variously what it is.

And so too after our hands cease
to pull the bucket from the well
in our tiny local sparkling place
as if it might be universal.

TEACHERS

I have met old teachers in strange places.
Some have had strokes, some play the violin
in a quiet little heaven of their own.
And some are standing on the banks of Hades
with books about Julius Caesar in their hands,
English grammar, absolute ablative.
Sometimes a huge wind blows them away,
the leaves of autumn. Sometimes in the snow
wearing their gowns of chalk they are writing.
I have met the old teachers in strange places
and there are apples trembling in their hands.

PUTTING OUT THE ASHES

A night such as we have never known,
millions of stars, shooting stars, a moon.
I stand and breathe the sky. It is breathing.
The supernatural light rests on the bin

freezing it to a palpable brilliant vase
from Greece perhaps, though it is packed with waste.
This is a marvellous spendthrift universe
a poet throwing off verse after verse.

HALLOWE'EN

This small child has an old man's face,
an old man's clayey bleak unquestioning face.
He plays the violin and sings a song,
small, expressionless, unquestioning.

And then after he has played he pulls
the mask away, and there he stands
fresh-faced and laughing with blonde curls
and from the grave extends his hands.

MACBETH AND THE WITCHES

When the sun was white and wintry and drained of energy
Macbeth met the witches under the rim of the sky.
Why did you confirm my evil, he said.

And the witches who were lighting thorns in the cold winter said,
There is a play that one plays when the summer is over
and you happened to be one of the cards in our hand,

a deformed king with a coat too large for him
and a crown that sizzled in the white wintry sky.
These things are after all not important

except to those who suffer, who are not important.
Feeling belongs to the spring and the ignorance of lovers.
Here in this wood it is a question of passing the time,

and the abstract intellect constructs dramas
with a queen and a pawn and the immortal joker
who faces two ways at the frosty January gates.

Let be, let be, it was quite a nice structure.
And truth after all can be played with under the sun
which is fading slowly towards a renaissance of leaves.

Come, join us, join us, at the unimportant edge of things
wearing your coat of blood with the hole in the breast.
This is the west. The east has innocent wings.

THE SPIDER

The spider's at the centre of the web
on this fine autumn day.
There he is clinging to our window pane.
Yesterday he crawled like an astronaut
breeding a line behind him,
or like a crab swaying through air not water.
He is not catching any flies.
He lives on air as poets do
and the justice of heaven.
The day is perfectly still,
a technique without ideas
as his web is,
a structure with nothing in it but itself.
To the quiet woods the cones are falling
and the trees are still on the hill.
What are you, spider, who are you
hunched brown and terrible
at the centre of your strands.
So much has been truly made,
the great responsible dead,
autumn so clean and pure,
and the fat spider
at his lean scant trade.

WELCOME

The sun is flashing from the hot gate.
Stranger, do not fear to come in.
There is cool water in the basin,
and there are shadows in the small rooms.
Remove your tunic and show yourself
entirely as the Muse,
who walks the dusty road in the summer.
            Please excuse
the tiles which are not marble,
the absence of statues from the hall.
But in the very depths of the hot garden
you will find an ordinary cool well.

THE GAELIC PROVERB

The Gaelic proverb says,
sad is the state of the house
without a child or cat.

But sad is the state of the child
who carries his house on his back
like a trapped snail.

And the cat who cannot go out
into the deep greenery
but sits on the spinster's lap,
narrow and infertile,
as the wild sun goes down.

NO MUSES

No, it's not a question of waiting for a voice from the sky
as in ancient days,

or sitting at a desk like Virgil while the empire prospered around him.

There is no such voice, objective and distant and impartial,
there are no Muses dressed in imperial blue.

It is more likely to be a flash from a piece of glass or from an old mirror,
it is more likely to be a squint-eyed man handing out crooked rifles at a fair,
it is more likely to be a girl swaying past in durable denims.

Virgil perfecting his lines in the seclusion of an eclogue
writing with a bronze pen about the golden outspread eagle,
did you believe in the gods, in Elysium and Hades?

For myself I have looked out of a train window
and seen a pheasant dressed in the tranquillity of stained glass
and I have heard an Ulsterman praising a blue church
set in a landscape of perishing rich green
and he was fat and loud-mouthed and he said, All Catholics are ugly,
and I have seen a child gazing into a well
beside a red gnome on an autumn morning.

And I have seen a wizened old woman standing greyly by a flourishing rose,

and a cat with emerald eyes stalking a robin:

and there is no calm glaze of an empire where I live
or praise for a bloodstained army fording a river
and seeing their red reflections in the water
and their pikes stuck up like a forest of branches
while the women squeal like rabbits in the undergrowth.

And a cool imperator sips from a glass of cold wine.

No, there is only the random kaleidoscope of images,
our wheel which knows no gods and is ignorant of fortune
and it is there that on a good day I labour

while the peasant bowed under his load trudges along a road
that does not lead particularly anywhere though the sun is hot on his shoulder.

MILTON

Out of the immense darkness your voice rose.
It was a fertile spring which defied
the excised stone, and the destruction of your hopes.
It wasn't the will, will cannot construct music,
which rises in solid pillar upon pillar,
to a new temple which was not built by hands.
You hear the louts and hooligans in the night
in their vanishing velvets and cold arrogance,
the wine guzzlers who splash blood on the wall,
those who have escaped the iron individualism of your planet –
yet the music will not cease in the moving darkness,
it creates Adam and Eve in their tremulousness,
it creates the devil elegant in snakelike green,
it creates a blitz of angels falling from the sky.
In spite of the destruction of hope, the music...
In your hebraic cloth, the holiness of your inspiration,
your head is an astronomy of stars, your ardour is relentless,
the music defies the darkness, and is heroic,
it renews itself endlessly in the reclusive silence of art.

Who cannot take comfort from you, old rancorous one
for whom the exact notation of nature was not enough,
for whom there were no real elegies even of the drowned?
You sing out of your blindness like a beggar,
at the extinct silence of your hopes you will not be silenced,
the holy doves perch on your scholarly shoulders
and common humanity is forgiven by your spartan star.
Your hearse is constructed of music
and your poems are as lasting as the towers of London,
its palaces and castles.
It is the bright architecture that soars out of the dark,

marvellous blind rancorous one who submitted your theology to death
and who are resurrected over and over in your music,
putting off the leaves, learning a classical bareness,
the handsome Apollo who wished to know all the rays of the sun
but who bumps in the end against the pillars of his own verse.

DREAM

Nervous, I carry my poems
to that chair
from which I read.

Around me
there are men in black masks,
women
with ambiguous laurels.

I speak.
My voice echoes
down the centuries
in competition with, say,
Lucretius.

I lift a huge weight.
My fingers shake,
corrupt compass needles.

O Lord,
let them relent,
smile.
Their harsh faces compose
no images of the rose.

Orpheus,
I am lost among the minerals
of the god of silver.

I rise.
The interview is over.

My poems fly
like the leaves of autumn away
to Vallombrosa.

I cry.
I break like rain
like a fine fresh April
composed of nuns,
shadows.

My masters
are still considering,
among a ring
of rocks and thistles.
Later they will tell me,
much later.

Perhaps when I am no longer here.

BOOKS

Books, what should I do
without you.
I should face
the meagre coarse
board of the world.
But with you,
sombre and true,
I inwardly digest
the rich feast
of learning. Rust
is far from me
as eased by you
I travel through
land after land
in which the gods burned
and the trees rose
shaggy and muscular,
tall and voluptuous,
from whose fine leaves
our pages are made.
O I'm arrayed
in brave dresses,
I am king
when I sit down and bring
your words closer.
Plots, dénouements,
stories and scents,
heroes and saints
these I always find
deep in these fond
gardens of yours –

all literatures.
Nor ever alone
am I, as down
the page my eye races
into your recesses.
Eternal fountains,
lovely philosophies,
brilliant legends,
and dry discourses.
Over-shadowing mountains,
my avid companions
who will not desert
me or my art
with your dry perfume,
calm autumn bloom.
I see my doom
as being always head-bent
over the page
to the very end
like a stone statue
which also has roses.
In the deepest crises
you comfort, you ease –
my allegories!
Tiny mirrors,
and miniature tombs,
you shine in my rooms,
unappeasable ones.
My loves, my true loves,
who will walk through the shades
with me, dear comrades,
without griefs, without griefs.

OTHERS

It is true that there are others... of course there are others around us,
like the receptionist who has to be patient in her cage,
or the garage mechanic who sets out in pouring rain to repair a car,
or the boy who went to a private school and though he wears glasses plays
rugby.
Or those who come to poetry readings and who ask no questions
or the gardener who works in the hot day in a cluster of flies
and who peers wistfully into the well where there is no water,
or the male teacher who endures the taunts of children and the
loveliness of the short-skirted mistress in the staffroom
or the newspaper seller who claps her hands in the bitter cold,
or the librarian who, tired of books, wishes someone would speak to her,
or the commissionaire with his blazing medals who stands in the evening like a
cockerel,
or the waitress who serves at table though her engagement has been broken
or the woman who stays with her daughter and son-in-law and wishes to be
alone
or the blind man who sings songs at an unforgiving corner.
All these there are and do not forget the air they inhabit
as your single will climbs the sky like a jet that's taking off from a shining
airport
and leaves an ashen mark on a sky of marvellous blue
as it sets off for Canada or Australia or Vietnam or any other country
where there are still more of the living centred in their loves and their work
and for whom the world is mainly themselves and their own shadows
and who stare up at the men with guns and the cold look of the tyrant
as the rain falls on the ricefields and on the soaked hats of the peasants
and there is autumn somewhere else breathtakingly beautiful
and the apples fall from the trees in the music of the fabulous nightingale.

AUTUMN

The sun shines on my desk.
Such joy, such joy it is
to work as if at music
on such clear autumn days.

When the rowans all in red
bend over water and
above the arranged dead
there is no breath of wind,

and eternity is this
tranquillity and poise
of orange-coloured trees
and flame-red bare displays

as if a visible fire
were an image of itself
both fact and its idea
trembling in double leaf.

from CONVERSION

7

Lord, I am waiting. Here is your perfect servant.
The breeze strays through the grass, the morning is cool.

I belong to the army of spirits that surrounds me.
On the mountain ahead of me, that bush is brilliant red,

an immortal poppy cleansed of ambiguous grief.
Our planes are travelling eastward towards the sun.

I belong to the hosts of God, invisible, pious.
My tunic sweats a little in this temporal wind

as once perhaps Joshua's seeing the land before him,
promised and dear. There is no undivided morning,

each is a bead hung on a historical chain.
Each is sacred with deeds, forgiven by justice,

the language of God is eternal, is Hebraic.
It is the black shadow cast on the steel of that tank.

Listen, I stand at attention before God,
the hum of His voice is persistent in my headphones

as the hum of that bee over that luminous flower.
Remember their hosts, their armies, their rancorous journey,

the wells where the angels bent down as into mirrors
to study their faces, imprints of passionate God.

I am ready, resolved. How shall the heart be passive
doglike or servile? God springs from the clouds,

eternal athlete, soldier, militant actor.
Soon I shall hear His voice, ardent and pure.

II

I bend and touch you, my enemies in the dawn.
Somewhere in this light the Idea explodes,

and rules, commandments, tablets, are blown away.
This grass appals our hitherto holy logic,

the minutiae of our testaments. I am here
alone, unsacred, in these early mists

swirling about my head. The sun will burn
soon like an armoured head. It is not God

nor our history's red helmet. It's the sun,
not jubilant or just, but the fire

natural in its socket of routine,
unwithering and distant. We shall soon

advance in our ponderous chains, prisoners
of symbol and of language, echoing forth

the voices of our power.
                                        We should not be
denunciatory prophets in this light

falling so helplessly around us all,
even on our enemies, now dead,

in their lucidity of pathos. Now it is,
the tents are lightening. It is time to stand

among these misty armies, it is time
not to defend the indefensible. We were mazed

by the heroes of our childhood. But the dream
of trumpets fades. I was caught

in a ruinous snare of history and books.
Now however there are human eyes

staring at me in this light and dew,
even my enemies. I'm a voyeur

of final uncluttered pure humanity.
I tremble like a leaf, I am freed

of symbol and of language. All I see
is Death the horse nibbling with stony teeth.

from THE HUMAN FACE

So therefore, human as we are,
in this vast theatre, whether 'star'
or extra in its great bazaar's
  dramatis personae
we're equal before nature's bare
  and rich arena.

As human beings, we are so,
beyond whatever dress we glow
in briefly: whether beau
  or tenement dweller,
whether we're Bardot or Monroe
  or Uri Geller.

Nature's indifferent to our ego.
Against its spacious imago
we're tiny, pitiful and meagre.
  That is the lesson
and the everlasting logos
  that human reason

must learn, for no one can be spared
from death's exuberant – not abhorred –
cupboard. And a ludicrous lord
  is the same to it
as a worker in Nissan or in Ford.
  Since we are set

in nature thus, in such a style,
dependent on each other's skill
an intricate factory or mill,
  a mutual body
that still is individual –
  Flora or Freddy –

which is more important then,
plumber or plasterer or en-
gineer, watchmaker or Gen-
  unine Tailor,
actor, actress, prince or sen-
  atorial

personage in a Parliament.
O let us hope that all consent
to see this transient tenement
  as our best home
and pay our individual rent.
  And though for some

not all is well, yet human kind
by such community entwined
may soon be brought to a refined
  correctness of seeing
and look without being wholly blind
  at the human being.

For as it is, the just, unjust,
the high, the low, may be reversed
and join the endless trails of dust
  of refugees,
the irremediably lost,
  in cold, disease.

And no political idea
on this small diminishing sphere
will save us till we *see*: and hear
  our brother's voice
human and pure and crystal clear
  beyond the noise

of radio, video, TV,
tills and polls and heresy,
the vicious demagoguery
  that fills our days,
the will to power, humbuggery,
  the ego's blaze.

from THE LEAF AND THE MARBLE

Part One: (1) The Green Leaf

My doughty one,
when I think of you
I think of light leaves in Rome
above the marble-
green leaves, green leaves!

As Michelangelo
on his shaky ladder
so I also admire
courageous fire
fiercely blossoming.

My love,
you believe
that luck will feed us
as meagre saints
hold out their gifts
from empty cupboards.

Not the statues,
no, not the statues,
those imperial riders –
no, but the green leaves
of early April.

Out of the darkness
I rise once more
putting on my blossoms,
and you are there,
a loyal candle.

In the hecatombs of Rome
and at Monte Cassino
so many of the dead,
the young, the ancient,
the crazed, the innocent,
whom the stone imprisons.

In the old damp walls
the martyred Christians.

But the Spring prevails
over the marble –
this shadow of the leaf,
this heartbreak green.

No, not the caparison
of majestic Caesar's
power-stricken hauteur.

But your frail moon,
wavering, shy,
over the dark Tiber.

The young wolves fed
at their lean dam

and I at times
have rested my rhymes
at your hopeful hostelry.

Courage, I am sure,
is the first of virtues

as among the libraries
of arid Ephesus
I saw the poppies
glowing among stones

or at Pompeii
among the ashes
a stubborn lion.

None shall be saved
who doesn't have courage.

As I am your judge
you have that power
which is beyond literature
and our screens of stories.

I come back again
to that bright green leaf
which is stronger than marble.

Rome may die,
as the slavering tribes
ache for its larder.
But that is all foam
if as the sun goes down
the emperor does not burn
in the light of love.

Let him recline
among spurious manuscripts,
how can he survive
in that acid air
of poisonous violins

without the passionate, clear,
gift of a companion.

So many statues,
heavy and firm.
So many riders
fixed in that stone
of determined time.

And the bridges tremble
among the daffodils.

Nevertheless
what without courage,
unwavering candle,
can be accomplished

as the dark Tiber
with its wolf-grey waves
is steadily flowing.

The leaf, the leaf!
April is here
with its constant shuttle.

And love is your
loyal imperative,
as hand in hand
we stroll through this grand

repertoire of scenes,

these pagan oracles
and pipe-playing fountains.

You pull me
out of
the deepest grave
with your bubbling music.
You do not let the antique
overwhelm you
or the helmets
of the dour legions

over whose shaded
and mortal faces
the green leaves play.

Play me my orchestra
of divine feeling
for April is here
and the grave is opened
and I see you there

my dear green leaf
which beyond art
is the gift of life.

O yes, O yes,
my hungry eyes
see this synthesis

though I do not despise
this weighty stone
from Carrara's shrine.

This leaf still plays
in front of the vast
marble arrays.

SHORTS

Drama Workshop

This is what I tell them about drama.
A stranger comes to the door
and the arranged plates fall off the walls.

Grass

The grass streams all one way
but there is no dénouement
to which it points.

Hallowe'en

They stood in silence
then removed their masks.
And below each mask there was another one.

Bus

There is no sorrow
worse than the sorrow
of seeing the last bus
draw away from the kerb.

Horse

Lackadaisically
it stares down at the ground

with its wealth of unbridled daisies.

Death

Come in, tall skeleton,
ladder of bones,

fold yourself into a chair,
and have a small sherry.

OLD LADY

I salute this gallant old lady
as I might a Roman heroine.

Protected by her Shakespeare
and her lovely classics
and her memories of a girls' school
she faces age with style.

She switches on the light
in a lonely house.
Daily through the window
she watches the leaves fall.

And she has a quotation from Shakespeare
with which to encounter death.

She will wear her quotations like a cloak
when he knocks on the door
and stands on the threshold
with, behind him, the moon.

A cup of coffee, she asks him
in her cool controlled voice,
you must be quite cold.

Is it as you like it?
she says remembering the wind
which blows through the leaves
of that Shakespearean play.

And she shivers a little
but retains her dignity
to the very end,

sitting quite upright
as the scythe-shaped moon
shines over the pale wood.

THE WINTER MOUNTAINS

Everywhere the white triangles of the snow
as if the local had become geometry
as if the deer had vanished into paper.

Triangles round us like real objects,
like Euclid's furniture staring out of the snow
in a polished glare as of intelligence

yet an alien stare also slightly bluish
with wilful shadows running over it
but no deer or flowers or leaves or stones.

As out of a book rises the white page
blatant, obvious, incurious,
whose shape will change though it does not know it yet.

NEIGHBOUR

Build me a bridge over the stream
to my neighbour's house
where he is standing in dungarees
in the fresh morning.

O ring of snowdrops
spread wherever you want
and you also blackbird
sing across the fences.

My neighbour, if the rain falls on you,
let it fall on me also
from the same black cloud
that does not recognise gates.

THE VOICE

The voice comes to me from deepest Ireland,
'I am safe, I am safe.'
It is midnight and the phone has just rung,
and the taxis are running to their termini
over the snake-blue lights.
'I am safe, I am safe,'
says the tiny voice with the rough accent
as of a stone climbing a hill forever.
There is eternal lightning among the churches,
a cross of green shining
to guide pedestrians over the abyss.
I am safe, safe, fixed forever in this minefield
of which my iron jacket is made,
of which my head is made and my heart is made.
The children fly through the skies like angels
with blood on their wings
and a man with broken knees stares in a pool
where he sees a rifle.
This is the Middle Ages again,
and the green leaves have blood on them
and Death with his scythe trots happily
up to what seems a safe ruby-coloured pane.

After the excitement in your head subsided
and you settled down in a landscape of grass and stone
you read your green Penguin detective stories.

The portrait of your flame-haired wife blazed above you
and dogs barked on the edge of the horizon
and planets shone in their aristocratic colours,

and the ghosts disappeared from thorn and thistle
and chimney smoke climbed straight into the air
and you lay on your white bed far from red Lenin.

ALL DAY

All day I have been reading.
I have lived inside books while the snow falls
very gently on the fields.
The mouse's small head is whitened
and the birds have a new weight on their wings.
I cannot stay inside this world forever.
Yesterday I saw an old man bowed in a chair
his face white with tedium and fear.
He was not able to read.
This was in a hospital
whose doors swung open and shut
faster than the pages of books.

THE VILLAGE

Above the village the dark clouds mass and gather.
The gates are open but no one comes in,
though they are painted yellow as the sun.
All one can hear is silence everywhere,

apart from one man digging with a spade
who is patiently planting his gardenias.
Now and again he lifts his pale face
and the poised weight of his rough thistly head.

And no one passes along the empty road
except for a lumbering black dog, heavy-jawed.

CHILDREN

One storms at the piano, one plays the computer,
and one sits quietly reading literature

and the roads outside the door point different ways
towards their changing Scotlands, Europes, Asias.

TWO WORLDS

The grandchildren fish the Internet while I
remember how it was in summer, sweatily

to play with a fishing cork on a full-sized pitch
just slightly northward of my becalmed cottage.

THE OLD MEN

On the dew on the faces of the young
and their hopefulness
the old men must not cast shadows.

For they remember how they would race
with a football along the wet grass
as if they were winged

and how spring leaves would touch the trams
as they set off in the morning
past devout cemeteries.

On the dew on the faces of the young
and their eyes which drink objects
and skies of early red mirrors

let the old men not cast shadows
or the knowledge of the depravities
which keep them at midnight awake.

SINCERITY WITHOUT ART

Sincerity without art
is not enduring.
Otherwise
would we not say
that 'In Memoriams'
are the summit of poetry.
'The heart'
what can 'the heart' say of itself
that is *aere perennius*.
Rather it should be cast in bronze
as on a Roman *via*
with a fountain
playing in the background
perhaps.
In stylish Italy
where even the poorest
know how to dress
and the screams from open mouths
are rimmed in luminous gold.

TIME TO STOP

It is time to stop writing about the Highland Clearances etc.

'O welcome to you, blue cuckoo, with your melodious sweet song.'

The cuckoo does not know the Highland Clearances
nor does the lark.

Yet they live here and perch on the gravestones and sing.

It is time to stop writing about the Highland Clearances.

The scythe-beaked golden eagle catches the sun
and does not see watery portraits in the lochs.

THE OLD WOMAN

It took me a while to push her down,
the old woman dressed in black, into the graveyard
and listen to the music of the wind.

And learn to love the ripe corn and stubble
and the voice of the young man who sang all day
and the horizon which cut the sky like a knife.

And the rainbow too I learned to love,
that lovely bridge which arches our fences
and the scholarly owl perched among trees.

And avenues of trees, greenly shaded,
and stones, wood, leaves, all these I learned to love
and to hate the honey colour of coffins.

And old women telling black stories
as they swayed in their unconditional dreams.

Island, rise up and put on a fresh music.

Put on your comic, not your mournful song
about horses with heads like varnished fiddles
and the Callanish Stones swathed in pink and blue.

PARKHEAD

How is it that these splendid stadiums
are planted among grimy streets
where the shop windows are boarded
and black graffiti sign sad clouds?

How is it that these buoyant players
weave their patterns on a ground
which is surrounded by dark houses
which sniffle with a dampish wind?

These roars as of a lion
emit the repression of seven days:
and rage at inherited injustice
pours downwards towards the fresh grass.

And scarves are stretched taut by supporters
at the beginning of the game:
'We are with you, our dear champions,
though ourselves we cannot save.'

Then you walk from that arena
towards your crouched houses again
and the closes with misspelt slogans
and the roofs which let in the rain

jaunty after victory
or desperate because of loss
you with the most intense passions
hanging on the destiny of a cross

happy-go-lucky fanatics
who thirst for a magical move
in the midst of deceits and ruins
and wages which run away, like love.

FOR EDWIN MORGAN

To swim out
into the impassioned light
and glint of the new,

as it seeks language
vulnerable, strange-spined,
blink-eyed

is for you mandatory.
Let the blue sky
bend over oddity

or even the monstrous –
The taste of poetry
is for you, this,

to substitute for the rose
in abandoned windows
the happy orphans.

OLD WOMAN

I see the old woman behind the flowering broom.
I have followed her from poem to poem

and her grey coat is almost hidden by that yellow and red
on a May day with white clouds overhead

billowing with pillows. Yes, she carries her bag
home from the village shop.
                                        And behind her a stag

in my imagination rears its magnificent head
out of the stones and flowers and small hills of the dead.

NOT A DAY FOR DANTE

This is not a day for Dante to visit me
and come in at the yellow gate.
The sky is overcast as it is not in Italy,
the rain smoulders on the hills.
I do not think he will like the cold
and this village is much smaller than Florence.
I suppose he could pull his cloak about him
as he mutters his three-lined verses.
There is no one here to be consigned to hell
and its mountains of flame
there is none here to be stirred about with a trident.
No the sky is too lowering.
But if you want to read a book I have plenty
and certainly I would refer to you
as to the greatest of masters.

HE SPOKE

He spoke as if from the other side of death
quite clearly and quite impressively.

I think from your side it is tragedy
but from my side here it's really comedy
dry, not furious but temperate.

The tables spread with goodies for the guest
in blazing uniform looks aslant at best

and so does the orator with his spurious crown.
Young, the slightest shame is tragedy,

Old, it is comedy and cause for laughter
in a pure red weather in the evening.

THE POET

I have outdistanced the music
I am travelling in silence
through the shadow of posthumous metres.

What my metres will be
will be what I shall become –

I am the skin-made drum

which the wind will fill.

AFTERWORD

It might be expected that someone born on New Year's Day would be keen to get on with things, and Iain Crichton Smith was somehow always associated with speed. He famously reviewed twenty-six crime novels in a single weekend, and his own classic *Consider the Lilies* was apparently the work of a fortnight. Even before he took early retirement from teaching he was writing compulsively – the twelve novels in English and Gaelic, a similar number of short story volumes, plays for stage and radio, translations, and innumerable poems. These came thick and fast, were seldom revised (he would rather throw a poem away 'and start on something else') and when he gave poetry readings, he rattled through them as if he was keen to get the next bus back to Argyll. They can be consumed quite quickly, too, almost at prose speed. Yet poems they undeniably are. As Robert Nye remarked in an article for *The Scotsman* (21/3/92):

> [Iain Crichton Smith] strikes me as an indubitably *inspired* poet, taking on the world in poem after poem, without once forgetting where his own roots go down and what he brings along with him to the task.

Those roots are important. No one who hoped to understand Wordsworth could separate that poet from the Lake District, and Iain Crichton Smith the man and the writer is inextricably tied up with the Isle of Lewis, even though he was in fact born in Glasgow.

His parents were native to Lewis, but had moved to the mainland because of John Smith's work as a Merchant Seaman.

When Iain was barely a year old his father died of TB and his mother took their sons back to the island, where she managed on a widow's pension of a pound a week in a house without plumbing or electricity. She was evidently a severe woman, single-minded in her Calvinism, yet he was always close to her, writing a series of love poems to her after her death. He was brought up with his two brothers in the aptly named village of Bayble, where the Gaelic-language poet Derick Thomson also lived (a friend, though from a more privileged background, commemorated in a fine sequence here). Bayble was the future poet's world, and in it he spoke Gaelic until he started school, where, devastatingly, only English was permitted in the classroom and indeed the playground. The family's straitened circumstances are as crucial as the place for a full understanding of the poetry. Young Iain Smith (the Crichton was only added when he began publishing in the 1940s) suffered from poor health and his mother was understandably protective; meals consisted of 'salt herring and potatoes every day except Sunday'. An annual visit to the cinema seven miles away in the 'capital', Stornoway, became the highlight of the year. If there were other happy or exciting moments (as the poem 'Some days were running legs' might suggest), this was no Eden such as Edwin Muir knew on Wyre.

A poet friend from the Western Isles explained to me how the islands differ: South Uist, for instance, is almost entirely Catholic, North Uist Protestant, whereas Lewis and Harris are predominantly Free Presbyterian 'and the Calvinist strain is a lot more strictly enforced than either religion on the Uists'. He makes Lewis in particular sound very distinct, very peculiar, and he told me he found it hard to imagine the claustrophobia of growing up in such a place. Even well into the twenty-first century, while the playgrounds are no longer chained up (except against coronavirus), there have been battles over Sabbath opening of playgrounds and swimming pools, and recently over ferry services. If such fundamentalism is weakening in the 2020s, during the 1930s there was no resistance: the hell-fire preachers and the hatred of art would have been enough to traumatize any child. Moreover, the poet's very birthday was also the anniversary of the island's most appalling tragedy, the wreck of the *Iolaire* on 1 January 1919, when an Admiralty yacht bringing men home from war for Hogmanay went down within hailing distance of the harbour. Over two hundred were drowned. Those many old women in the poems are partly mythological, the *Cailleach*; they are also a reminder of the number of widows on the island. Lewis is said to have suffered the UK's highest losses as a proportion of population

Iain Crichton Smith's life was in other respects apparently unremarkable and he was little involved with wider politics, although much of what he writes has a political dimension, not least because of his Gaelic-speaking background. 'To write in English,' he says in his prose book *Towards the Human* (1986), 'becomes a form of treachery'. Recent critics have even interpreted his poems about tension between generations (e.g.'It is the old') as allegories of colonialism. He himself used the term 'interior colonisation' in writing of the tendency among Gaels to 'believe that the English world must be presumed to be more important'. Nevertheless, as James Campbell put it in a *TLS* tribute, for Iain Crichton Smith 'the big event was literature, and the movers of history were as likely to be fictional, or mythic, as real'. It must have been extraordinary for him to leave Lewis for the first time, with a love of literature (especially Auden) and of the Classics (especially Homer), to study English in Aberdeen, as described in an early poem not included in this selection:

> Mica glittered from the white stone.
> Town of the pure crystal,

> I learnt Latin in your sparkling cage,
> I loved your brilliant streets.

He had never seen a train before, and to meet a blind beggar as he got out of the carriage was a new, unsettling experience. In one of his Gaelic poems, 'To My Mother', he thinks of how his mother at the same age had been a 'herring girl' down on the English coast:

> You were gutting herring in distant Yarmouth and the salt sun in the morning rising out of the sea, the blood on the edge of your knife, and that salt so coarse that it stopped you from speaking and made your lips bitter.
>
> I was in Aberdeen sucking new courses, my Gaelic in a book and my Latin at the tiller, sitting there on a chair with my coffee beside me and leaves shaking the sails of scholarship and my intelligence.
>
> Guilt is tormenting me because of what happened and how things are. I would not like to be getting up in the darkness of the day gutting and tearing the fish of the morning on the shore and that savage sea to be roaring down my gloves without cease.
>
> Though I do that in my poetry it is my own blood that is on my hands, and every herring that the high tide gave me palpitating till I make a song, and instead of a cooper my language always hard and strict on me, and the coarse salt on my ring bringing animation to death.

After university, Crichton Smith trained as a teacher at Jordanhill College, Glasgow, but had to go through National Service from 1950–52, serving as a sergeant in the British Army Education Corps. He then taught in schools for many years (one of the things that prompts a feeling of kinship in his current editor) while living less than harmoniously with his mother and becoming increasingly well known both in

Scotland and beyond. There would eventually be numerous awards, several honorary degrees and an OBE, but first came the ordeal of teaching in Clydebank. There followed two decades in the rather happier Oban, although his mother became once again a looming presence in the last years of her life. One story he related to Colin Nicholson suggests the difficulty of living with a Free Church fundamentalist. He had been to see a film in Oban and heard his mother speaking with another old woman, who was saying:

> 'That was a terrible thing there,' and I thought they were talking about the starving millions of India which had been the subject of the film. But they were talking about the fact that the minister had put the film on in the church hall. The starving millions had made no impression on them at all. I thought again, 'My God, if there's a religion that can create that kind of effect in people then there must be something definitely wrong with it.'

As a boy, he had been reprimanded by her for making model hens ('Why do you make wooden hens when the Lord has made real ones?') and evidently she had still not mellowed. It was only some years after her death that he was able to give up teaching (in 1977), which was also when he married Donalda Gillies Logan – and became a stepfather.

What was not generally known until the 1990s is that Iain Crichton Smith had suffered a breakdown when he was 57 (the experience fed into his novel, *In the Middle of a Dark Wood*). His long silence on this is significant in itself and contrasts with the public collapse of certain American poets, but he began to open up when his *Collected Poems* appeared in 1992. Talking with Catherine Deveney for *Scotland on Sunday* six years later, he described how one day he had simply picked up his typewriter and headed for the train (followed by Donalda 'without whom he says he never would have survived') and woke in a Glasgow hotel with a man leaning over him saying 'I am Dr Emmanuel'. He was unable to recognise what was real and what fantasy, 'as if reality was shimmering in front of me, changing shape'. He put it down to overwork (Norman MacCaig had famously joked that he was worried about Iain as he hadn't published a book for days) and to the stress of moving from Oban to Taynuilt, a village near Loch Etive, in 1982. But in an interview for his seventieth birthday only a few months before his death (available in *The Dark Horse* magazine's online archive), he suggested to Gerry Cambridge that it had stemmed from the trauma of rejecting the dogma of his upbringing, 'moving out into the open sea' as he put it. He added that the chief effect was that he 'joined the human race'. Only after that do we find phrases like 'such joy, such joy' in the poetry, and a capacity for sheer praise (in 'The Leaf and the Marble') unprecedented in modern British poetry – reading the *Selected Poems* can feel like a journey from darkness into light.

There are other such recurrent phrases in Iain Crichton Smith's collections, certain gestures (look how many poems begin with a forthright, steadying definite article) and many favourite nouns: mirror, deer, book, rose, scholar, vase, clock, snow, Rome, sea, autumn, sun, marble. Some of these take on the authority of archetypes, and some of them return obsessively – that ubiquitous old woman, for example, the Gaelic Matriarch; but there is her opposite too, the young girl. Those 'Two Girls Singing' are surely descendants of Wordsworth's 'solitary highland lass', the representative of hope and escape from darkness, a kind of purity. Tension between 'the Law and the Grace' (title of an early collection) is repeatedly evident and is made the more potent by the poet's self-confessed and perhaps schoolmasterly ambivalence towards puritanical codes of behaviour – 'Roman values' as he calls them, exemplified by the Oban scholar and headmaster,

John Maclean. At root, the distinction is a Biblical one ('the Law was given by Moses, but grace and truth came from Jesus Christ'), and it lies behind many of Crichton Smith's other 'paired' titles from *Thistles and Roses* in 1961 to *The Leaf and the Marble* in the year of his death. The struggle is between dogma and something powerfully liberating, which the critic John Blackburn defines as 'that sense of inner harmony and beauty which can suddenly take possession of us ... but also an upsurge of well-wishing towards another living thing.' For example, in a very late long poem, 'Conversion', from which only an extract has been possible here, the poet takes us to the Arab-Israeli conflict and imagines a kind of resolution as the zealous fighter sees the bodies of his victims, the victims of blind belief, and his heart softens: 'I bend and touch you, my enemies in the dawn./Somewhere in this light the Idea explodes,//and rules, commandments, tablets, are blown away.' Michael Schmidt, alluding to this ambitious formal experiment, notes that the poet is 'compelled into the action he can undertake, which is to write not out of security and safety but out of risk', adding that Crichton Smith takes aesthetic risks by eschewing irony: he will 'keep a poem if he feels it tells, however marred it may be, a valuable part of a truth'.

Another abiding concern is exile, something Crichton Smith believed was connected to his bilingual upbringing, as he explained to Gerry Cambridge:

> I think I feel that if the Gaelic had been stronger when I was younger I would have been writing in Gaelic all the time. So I'm exiled from that and the ideology in which I grew up. I also feel a terrible sense of waste, that a lot of the people from the islands had to leave the islands to go to places like Canada, and so forth. Many of them became alcoholics, many of them died of starvation. There was a lot of wastage of really good people. From my own family, just to show what exile was like, I had an uncle

> who was in South Africa, another uncle who was in Vancouver in Canada, an aunt in Fort William in Canada, a cousin who had been in Canada and came back home. My older brother spent most of his life in Rhodesia, later Zimbabwe, and my younger brother went to New Zealand and died in Australia. So my whole family was full of people who left, and stayed away.

But there are other preoccupations: simple ones like a love of Shakespeare, an interest in the world of school-teaching, a fascination with colours (yellow in the early poems seems to represent something disturbing), a suspicion of television, a relish for debate; or complex ones such as the history and condition of Scotland – and indeed the wider human condition in *The Human Face* (1996). This ambitious and not wholly successful book-length experiment with the Burns stanza (Robert Nye's review was ominously headlined 'Second Degree Burns') inhabits similar territory to Lowell's *Near the Ocean*. Iain Crichton Smith became more experimental as he got older, and like his admired 'free spirit' Auden could probably write a poem on anything asked of him in any given form and make it look easy.

In fact, many of his poems turn out to be about poetry itself, and this tendency became more overt in Crichton Smith's final books. But it is also true of his masterpiece 'Deer on the High Hills' (1962), a work which came to him unexpectedly – rather, one feels, as *The Rite of Spring* came to Stravinsky – and at a point in his development when there was a fruitful tension between the formal and the free. Deer are a traditional symbol of grace, as Carol Gow points out in her study of his poetry, *Mirror and Marble*. She claims that in this poem he 'becomes a poet of major status', undermining the 'created grace' of his earlier 'brilliant metaphor and dazzling language' to reach a new imaginative level as 'discoverer of his own meanings, reader of his own work'. Iain Crichton

Smith spotted these particular deer by the side of the road one night while he was driving home from Glasgow. He had been reading Dante, which must have affected his choice of verse form, and somewhere at the back of his mind too was the Gaelic poetry of Duncan Ban MacIntyre who, as Crichton Smith writes in 'Light to Light' (not included here) 'saw the deer moving waxen-skinned/in a light that is not our light,/ the light of love./That equable happy and cheerful man/who shot the deer with poetry.' Although he originally called it 'a Meditation', Carol Gow tells us that 'Deer on the High Hills' was written quickly:

> and he confesses that he finds it a strange poem, one that he cannot account for or fully understand, though he recognises its importance. What is important, perhaps, to Crichton Smith, is that the poem seems to be unauthorised, to come from that part of the creative impulse which he has termed the 'imagination'

She then quotes his remarks on the mystery of imagination, how it is 'what we require in poetry at the highest level' although 'how it operates is incomprehensible'. Nevertheless, the poet has offered convincing explanations elsewhere, suggesting to Colin Nicholson, for example, that 'the best poetry happens when two or three things come together which one would normally think of as being totally unrelated ... Scientists do this too. It's the kind of leap that changes something at deep levels, so that we can start thinking in a new way.' In the same interview, he explained his interest in following the 'logic of images', which he learnt from *The Waste Land*.

From the start, Iain Crichton Smith was conscious that the very act of composition would be a challenge to Bayble puritanism. In what could be called his signature piece, the 'Poem of Lewis', he writes of the island community's intolerance for 'the fine graces/of poetry, unless it freely grows/in deep compulsion' – that is to say, unless it is popular balladry, or something like the Gaelic verses of Duncan Ban McIntyre. Crichton Smith's early poems are usually formal, precisely metred (significantly, he has spoken of metre as a 'cage'). But he often wrong-foots the reader in unexpected ways, disrupting what appeared to be a pattern, trusting grace rather than law. The poems of the fifties and early sixties owe much to the Metaphysicals (see, for example, 'A Young Highland Girl Studying Poetry' from 1961, with its play on the 'little death' of sexual consummation) and to certain fashionable Americans such as Robert Lowell – though Richard Eberhart's 'The Groundhog' is surely behind 'Sunday Morning Walk'. Sometimes he will confront an historical figure – Lenin or Hume or Johnson – and thrash out the issues. There are a number of powerful elegies for which the metrical precision is especially apt, the finest being his great suite of funeral music for the classical scholar John Maclean (1909–70)*, Rector of Oban High School where Crichton Smith taught, and brother of the Gaelic-language poet Sorley MacLean whose 'Dàin do Eimhir' had affected him profoundly as a teenager on Lewis. This new *Selected* did not seem the place for his fine translations of 'Poems to Eimhir', but they can be found in the Carcanet *New Collected*.

In subsequent decades Iain Crichton Smith took the considerable risk of casting off metre and almost doing away with metaphor too (again, this is like many American poets of the period from James Wright to Adrienne Rich). 'Deer on the High Hills' prepares the ground for the coming plainness:

> There is no metaphor. The stone is stony.
> The deer step out in isolated air.
> We move at random on an innocent journey.

---

* Unlike Sorley, John Maclean did not capitalise the 'l' of his surname.

The rain is rainy and the sun is sunny.
The flower is flowery and the sea is salty.
My friend himself, himself my enemy.

Although he was continually drawn back to strict forms for big occasions, elegiac commemorations ('Photograph of Emigrants' in the late eighties), as well as for the purposes of experiment ('The Human Face' in the nineties), the general direction of travel was towards a *vers* that was more *libre*. Talking to Colin Nicholson, Crichton Smith suggested that the austere landscape and religion of Lewis itself acted 'as a kind of honing for what I'm doing'. There is inevitably a great deal of wastage with this approach, but when the plain style finds the groove, it is unbeatable and there are many poems from the 1970s that have barely dated in either their concerns or their language. Very often there is a little story that holds the poem together. Or a character. He likes to open with a 'you', speaking directly perhaps to a friend or relative, a figure from history or indeed from fiction. At one point, successive poems in this selection are addressed to John Maclean, Hamlet, various Russians and John Keats. He enjoys dramatic monologues too, putting himself into the mind of an adulterous wife ('In the Glen'), a baby ('Incubator'), a schoolboy ('Rythm') or that soldier in Palestine (Conversion'). He was keen for poets to engage with major public issues (his own first poem at the age of eleven – in Gaelic and composed orally – was about Neville Chamberlain's meeting with Hitler) and he felt increasingly that there had been a retreat from that responsibility. He also sensed that his contemporaries had lost their ear. It was in one of his last essays for the Scottish magazine *Chapman* that he wrote of the need for 'a new music in poetry. Not a new imagery but a new music.'

As I mentioned in the foreword, my wife and I heard Iain Crichton Smith read just the once, when he was invited to

Dundee by Douglas Dunn to launch his second *Selected Poems* (edited by Robin Fulton). I recall Douglas emphasising what an important occasion it was. It felt important, and it's one of the highlights of our time living in North East Scotland, just before I fell into the career of school-teaching from which he had finally liberated himself. But I suspect that he enjoyed the teaching as much as I did (somewhat grudgingly), and that he was a fine teacher. He was certainly a very entertaining performer, 'a glorious stand-up entertainer with a dry, dead-pan delivery who was never happier than when reducing his audience to helpless laughter,' according to Colin Nicholson (in *Fivefathers,* 2007). His reading of the brilliantly Arthur Waley-esque 'Chinese Poem', still rings in my ears, and some of his anecdotes – such as the one about the local man so dedicated to laying new trackways that he was known as the 'Colossus of Roads'. Nicholson describes Crichton Smith's hilarious turn at Norman MacCaig's 75th birthday party, where he read one of his own very popular Murdo stories. He makes a persuasive case for the importance of these comic pieces and relates them to Crichton Smith's vision of himself in one of his Gaelic poems, 'The Fool':

> In the dress of the fool, the two colours that have tormented me – English and Gaelic, black and red, the court of injustice, the reason for my anger, and that fine rain from the mountains and these grievous storms from my mind streaming the two colours together so that I will go with poor sight in the one colour that is so odd that the King himself will not understand my conversation.

James Campbell uses this same translation as epigraph to a chapter in his *Invisible Country* (1984) where he describes an eight hour conversation in Oban with the poet (whisky was also present). It gives as good an impression as any of the man as I remember him when he came to Dundee: 'slight, with a bald head and bright eyes', his face 'ready and youthful', his steep forehead 'occasionally worried by a concertina brow'. Campbell notes that he was very precise in his speech ('occasionally' would have 'six clear syllables'), very imprecise in his dress, shaving and typing. He is struck particularly by the 'absence of self-importance'. He also notes the sheer anger he expressed towards the Free Church. His last words to Campbell were 'Do you not, like me, get more and more bewildered by the ... multi-far-i-ous-ness of things?'

But reading and re-reading all the collections, what strikes me now is Iain Crichton Smith's understanding of and sympathy for other human beings. He himself had 'flown through darkness towards joy', but the poems engage with issues of poverty and suffering in a way which is rare today. How does he manage in 'Girl and Child' or 'Poor Artist', for example, to convey his heartfelt understanding? This after all is the same poet who is so cynical about Christmas and so-called Christian values. It is the same poet who can ask coolly a few pages earlier how anyone can possibly survive if they don't have talent. It is that combination of the icily accurate observation and the warmth of fellow feeling that makes him so memorable, although none of it would matter if he did not also have such a gift for the music of the language – indeed, of two languages.

Crichton Smith's death from throat cancer was predictably swift – within five weeks of the diagnosis according to Angus Calder's obituary in the *Independent*. 'The Bible got him at last,' he wrote. 'Exactly three score years and ten.' *The Times* described how shortly before the end he was visited by a friend in Taynuilt. The poet 'pointed to his unfinished autobiography: "It only covers the first 35 years, I'm afraid – the boring bit."' The commemorative articles were full of such anecdotes. Alan Riach, whose father went to school with him, wrote in *PN Review* 'How could one feel anything but liking for a man who said that, when he saw a Free Church minister walking on the other side of the road, he felt he must physically restrain himself from crossing over to knock him on the head?' And there were elegies, as I have already mentioned, by Seamus Heaney and other poets who regarded him as a poetic father figure. Robert Crawford, in 'Ceud Mile Failte' ('a hundred thousand welcomes') movingly imagined him transformed into a silkie, its head 'hazel-bald and polished', and then floating through the doorway of a white house, 'Chatting with your friends in one room in English,//Calling to the others in Gaelic.'

SELECT BIBLIOGRAPHY

Blackburn, John, *The Poetry of Iain Crichton Smith* (Glasgow: Association for Scottish Studies, 1993) [see also the CD, *15 Poems of Iain Crichton Smith: a Commentary by John Blackburn*, Association for Scottish Literary Studies, 2008]

Campbell, James, *Invisible Country, A Journey Through Scotland* (London: Weidenfeld & Nicolson, 1984)

Crawford, Robert, 'Ceud Mile Failte', *The Tip of My Tongue* (Cape, 2003)

Day, Gary and Dochery, Brian (ed.), *British Poetry from the 1950s to the 1990s*: Politics and Art, ed. Gary Day & Brian Docherty (Basingstoke: Macmillan Press, 1997 [the chapter by Colin Milton 'Half of My Seeing: the English Poetry of Iain Crichton Smith']

Gow, Carol, *Mirror and Marble: The Poetry of Iain Crichton Smith* (Edinburgh: Lines Review Editions, The Saltire Society, 1992)

Lindsay, Maurice (ed.), *As I Remember: Ten Scottish Authors Recall How for Them Writing Began* (London: Robert Hale, 1979)

Mitchell, Andrew, *Taking you Home: Poems and Conversations* (Glendaruel: Argyll Publishing, 2006)

Nicholson, Colin, *Fivefathers: Interviews with late Twentieth Century Scottish Poets* (Humanities-Ebooks, 2010)

Smith, Iain Crichton, *New Collected Poems* (Manchester: Carcanet Press, 2011)

—*A Country for Old Men* and *My Canadian Uncle* (Manchester: Carcanet Press, 2000)

—*The Human Face* (Manchester: Carcanet Press, 1996)

—*Ends & Beginnings* (Manchester: Carcanet Press, 1994)
—*Selected Poems* (Manchester: Carcanet Press, 1982)
—*Selected Poems 1955-1980* (Loanhead, Midlothian: Macdonald Publishers, 1981)
—*Towards the Human: Selected Essays* (Edinburgh: Lines Review Editions, The Saltire Society, 1986)
Wilson, Grant. F., *A Bibliography of Iain Crichton Smith* (Aberdeen: Aberdeen University Press, 1990)

INDEX OF POEM TITLES